The Mitchell Beazley Birdwatcher's Pocket Guide

Peter Hayman

Mitchell Beazley Publishers Limited, London
in association with
The Royal Society for the Protection of Birds

Birdwatching Basics

Birds are the most fascinating, varied and obtrusive of the wildlife around us, and ornithology the most popular and sophisticated of our wildlife sciences. You do not need, however, to lavish great expense on books and equipment to enjoy birdwatching. All you need is a pocket guide, pencil, notebook and pair of binoculars.

Before dashing out into the sunrise, the prospective birdwatcher should first sit down and browse through his guide, as far as possible familiarizing himself from his armchair with the commoner species. In the field, look first at size, making a rough guess as to whether the bird is sparrow-, blackbird- or crow-sized to help the process of elimination. This first step, it must be said, is fraught with difficulties—distance and light can beguile even the expert. Birds often look larger than they are and, in general, the farther north one goes, the brighter and larger are the individuals of any species. Next look at colouring, alert for the highlights of colour or pattern which strike the eye—such features are emphasized visually and verbally in the following pages. Behaviour and voice provide further pointers. However, both these aspects can be misleading; birds, like all other creatures, often behave unaccountably, and song and calls are difficult to distinguish and remember, and even more difficult to interpret from a book. After making your observation, check the habitat against the guide or make a note of it. The bird should be in roughly the right place at the right time, although great overlaps of habitat occur, and wind, weather and migration can land a bird in strange places.

Confident identification of the commoner and more distinctive species quickly becomes second nature, leaving greater opportunity for study of birds that are less frequently encountered or more difficult to identify. However, experience does not remove the pitfalls or change basic truths. Birds do not always run to type. Plumage, as well as varying greatly from individual to individual, in general gets duller as the year progresses towards the pre-winter moult. Populations can also alter radically, either in numbers or distribution, as changes in climate or habitat have their effect. Such factors apparently conspire to make identification more difficult, but they also add to the variety and richness of the avifauna.

Finally, how you act yourself will greatly affect how much birdlife you and others out with you will see. Follow the country code in general, and go quietly during the breeding season in particular, disturbing the birds and their habitat as little as possible and keeping well away from nests. With these hints and the information in the following pages, it should be possible to identify almost any bird seen in a lifetime of walks in town and country. Most important of all, watch birds in the way that you enjoy best, be it listening, listing, note-taking, counting or just plain watching.

Edited and designed by
Mitchell Beazley Publishers Limited
14-15 Manette Street, London W1V 5LB

ISBN 0 85533 1488

Typeset in Great Britain by Vantage Group, London
Colour Reproduction by Culver Graphics, High Wycombe, Bucks
Produced by Mandarin Offset   Printed and bound in Hong Kong
Editor Chris Phillips   Editorial Assistant Susanne Haines
Art Editor Linda Francis   Designer Colin Salmon

How the Guide Works

The *Birdwatcher's Pocket Guide* is dedicated to the idea that birdwatching is about observing birds and not about consulting books, so it has been designed to give the most complete picture of each bird in the simplest, quickest way possible. Bird identification does not usually depend on spotting a single feature, but on noting size, shape, plumage, behaviour, even facial expression in order to gain an overall impression. The illustrations in this book are designed to convey the many different aspects of character, appearance and behaviour which identify each species. All birds illustrated are adult unless otherwise indicated, and male and female are only distinguished if they differ in appearance. The text supplies any information not carried visually, such as call, and gives further facts about behaviour, numbers and distribution. Birds are grouped by resemblance; find a bird similar to the one being observed, then use a process of elimination until the right species is pinpointed. The species are divided into perching birds, game birds, predators and water birds, and within each of these groups are dealt with in roughly ascending order of size. The bird outlines on page 192 show how best to record salient features.

Woodchat

Unique chestnut crown

Typical view of perched birds

White rump and outer tail

White

Juv

♀

At rest and in flight, juv shows shadow of adult plumage. Shape is also diagnostic ▸

♀ and juv have duller version of ♂'s pattern ▸

Juv

Rounder-headed, broader-winged and shorter-tailed shrike than Red-backed species. Adult plumage is unmistakable and juvenile is always identifiable by shape, especially of head, bill and tail.

Symbols show status and habitat—(see key)

Species silhouette (left) shows size against a sparrow or a pigeon (see key)

Annotation emphasizes diagnostic features

Illustrations show typical plumage, attitude and behaviour

Text expands on the information in the illustrations. Key identifying features are italicized

 Any built-up area; parks, gardens; industrial sites

 Any freshwater including ditches, dykes and marsh

 Seaside and environs including estuaries

 All farmland, arable pasture, orchard or coppice; farm buildings

 All forests; plantations, open park and forest

 Very low vegetation (up to 1 metre); bare ground, moorland and maquis

 Low base vegetation, with or without scattered trees up to 10 metres

(R 60) Resident (i.e. non-migratory) in British Isles and among 60 commonest species

(S 60) Summer migrant and one of our 60 commonest species

(W 60) Winter migrant and one of our 60 commonest species

(S) Summer migrant (migrating north from Africa to breed in European summer)

(W) Winter migrant (breeds farther north or east and migrates south or west)

(R) Resident in British Isles throughout the year

(RV) Very rare or vagrant species

(P) Passage migrant, usually in spring or autumn

  ♂♀ Sparrow silhouette

   ♂♀ Pigeon silhouette

Species List

Birdwatching covers in a concise way every species that the average amateur naturalist could reasonably expect to come across in a lifetime of watching birds in the British Isles. The book's 350 birds include every one of our 220 breeding species, all regular summer and winter visitors and passage migrants, as well as a number of those "ornithological windfalls" that occasionally cross our shores.

The visitor to mainland Europe will find all the species normally encountered within an arc described from Murmansk, through Warsaw to Biarritz, so encompassing the avifauna of western Europe.

Because this book was designed above all to aid identification, we have not classified birds by evolutionary relationship as is conventional. Accidents of climate and geology and the simple necessities of survival often make closely related birds very different, while convergent paths of evolution can create beguiling similarities in birds that are completely unrelated. Birds are grouped solely by their similarity of appearance, size and habitat, with the most similar birds appearing side by side for instant comparison of their distinguishing features. The species are listed alphabetically here for ease of reference; see key to symbols on page 6.

Key

*Birds that breed in the British Isles
†Birds not seen in the British Isles
Italic type The ten commonest species in the British Isles

Terminology and Abbreviations

Technical terms have been used extremely sparingly; and the bird outline
and key on page 192 shows clearly to which part of the bird any
ornithological term refers. Where distribution is described, Britain
includes England, Wales, Scotland and outlying islands, while the British
Isles includes Britain and Ireland.

Abbreviations used are: ♂ = male; ♀ = female; sp(p) = species (plural);
juv = juvenile; imm = immature; esp = especially; cp = compare.

Acknowledgements

Useful and authoritative publications, to which the author is particularly
indebted are:
British Birds (Macmillan Journals Ltd., monthly magazine)
Cramp, S. & Simmons, K. E. L., *The Birds of the Western Palearctic*
(O.U.P., 1977)
Sharrock, J. T. R., *The Atlas of Breeding Birds in Britain and Ireland* (T. &
A. D. Poyser, 1977)
Sharrock, J. T. R. & E. M., *Rare Birds in Britain and Ireland* (T. & A. D.
Poyser, 1976)

Goldcrest

Firecrest

Both species have yellow crowns, which are spread in display to reveal the orange feathers

Goldcrest

Minute-looking in flight, with short, rounded wings and slightly forked tail. Note the double white bars and black patch on wing

Goldcrest

Goldcrest has prominent, beady black eye set in pale face, with black stripe above and yellow crown. Seen full face, this combination makes the bird unmistakable

Pale face

Goldcrest

Extent of white

Firecrest

Firecrest's bold white eye stripe between 2 black stripes gives it a quite different look. Nape is copper coloured

Both species are agile feeders, and can hover to catch flying insects or pick aphids from the underside of leaves

The smallest of all the European birds, the Firecrest and Goldcrest share very similar habits. They mainly feed high in trees (especially conifers), but may also hunt among low vegetation and bushes. In winter they often join roving parties of tits. Can be extremely tame. Goldcrest has shrill, insistent "zee-zee-zee" call. Song is a thin, high double note ending in a short twitter. Firecrest is best located by crescendo of increasingly fast "zit" notes. Goldcrest is common throughout British Isles, but Firecrest population is very small, with only about 20 breeding areas (especially in tall Norway spruce) S of line between Severn and Wash. Isolated passage and wintering birds occur.

Wren

Flight is direct, whirring and fast

There are usually 2 broods of 6 young

Cocked tail

Slightly curved bill

Pale eye stripe

Picking for insects in typical "creeping", crouching posture

Nest may be in recess in tree, ivy or bank

Brownish upperparts, greyish underparts and quick, jerky movements create *mouse-like appearance*. Often to be seen on a branch *bobbing* confidently with *tail cocked*. Loud, scolding "tit-tit-tit" call often changing to a "churring" note. Song loud and explosive. Commonest bird of all and found everywhere, but severely hit by hard winters.

Dunnock

Grey head

Thin bill

Streaking (cp Sparrow)

Wing-bar sometimes absent

Superficially sparrow-like, but grey head and underparts, streaked buff flanks, fine bill and orange eye are distinctive

Flight is unhurried and undulating. Grey head and streaked back often show well

Dunnock "creeps" over ground when foraging for mites

♂ flicks each wing in turn in unique spring courtship display

A *quieter, more demure species than the ubiquitous sparrow*. It will be seen in gardens and scrubland picking delicately for food, moving in slow, shuffling hops. *Frequently flicks wings and tail*. Call, a high, piping "tseep" and trilling note. Song, a pleasant warble heard all year round. Common throughout the British Isles.

Tree Sparrow

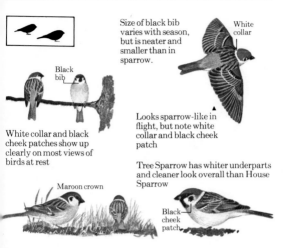

Size of black bib varies with season, but is neater and smaller than in sparrow.

White collar

Black bib

White collar and black cheek patches show up clearly on most views of birds at rest

Looks sparrow-like in flight, but note white collar and black cheek patch

Tree Sparrow has whiter underparts and cleaner look overall than House Sparrow

Maroon crown

Black cheek patch

Distinctly *smaller, more compact in appearance and shyer than the sparrow. Sexes are alike.* Picks quietly on ground for food. Nests in tree holes and, more rarely, buildings. Flight direct like sparrow. Call, a short, sharp "chup" and "tek-tek" on wing. Fairly common, but often overlooked. Not found in towns. Absent much of Scotland, W Wales and Ireland.

House Sparrow

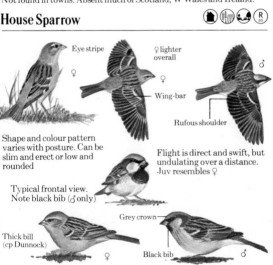

Eye stripe

♀ lighter overall

♀

♂

Wing-bar

Rufous shoulder

Shape and colour pattern varies with posture. Can be slim and erect or low and rounded

Flight is direct and swift, but undulating over a distance. Juv resembles ♀

Typical frontal view. Note black bib (♂ only)

Grey crown

Thick bill (cp Dunnock)

♀

Black bib

♂

Cheeky, aggressive, garrulous bird. Goes wherever man goes and almost always breeds in buildings. Catholic appetite. Often tries, usually unsuccessfully, to catch insects on the wing. Town birds dingier than country birds. Builds untidy nest in wall cavities, hedges or ivy. Chirruping calls but no song. Common throughout British Isles.

Coal Tit

White cheeks

Forked tail

Thin bill

Disproportionately large head, glossy black crown, white cheeks and nape, and warm buff belly plumage distinguish the Coal Tit. Grey-brown back of British race contrasts with blue-grey of continental race

Nape patch

◀ Adult collecting beech mast

Black bib

Irish race has yellow-buff cheeks and buff nape which show clearly in feeding

Juv is drab with yellower face, nape and belly

The smallest British tit (less than half Great Tit's weight) and typically restless and acrobatic. Stores food. White wing-bars are evident in its fast, flitting flight. Call, a thin, clear "tsui", also "susi-susi". Song, a clear, repeated "seetoo-seetoo". Common in British Isles (especially among conifers). Visits gardens and nut bags.

Crested Tit

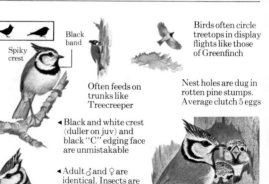

Spiky crest

Black band

Often feeds on trunks like Treecreeper

◀ Black and white crest (duller on juv) and black "C" edging face are unmistakable

◀ Adult ♂ and ♀ are identical. Insects are picked from pine needles with fine bill

Birds often circle treetops in display flights like those of Greenfinch

Nest holes are dug in rotten pine stumps. Average clutch 5 eggs

Only small bird with a crest to occur in Britain; restricted to natural pine woods in central N Scotland. Whitish underparts, brown upperparts and head pattern are unique. A typical tit, restless and acrobatic. Stores food. Trilling call betrays its presence; also has thin "tzee-tzee-tzee" call. Widely distributed on Continent.

Willow Tit

Marsh Tit

Head is larger and cap longer and less glossy

Crown feathers can be very glossy and bird has no wing panel

Willow Tit

Pale wing panel (less obvious in summer)

◀ Bull-headed, puff-cheeked look of Willow Tit is best guide to the difference. Marsh Tit has a rounder head and is browner

Bull-necked look of Willow Tit still obvious from back. Marsh Tit is clearly slimmer

Scandinavian race of the Willow Tit has white cheeks and a grey back

Marsh Tit

Marsh Tits use natural nest holes and do not excavate their own like the Willow Tit

Diagram shows difference in size and shape of head

Willow Tit

Typical Willow Tit profile

Typical Marsh Tit profile

Marsh Tit

Two species rarely occur together so comparison is virtually impossible. Identification largely depends on view obtained and is very difficult in Britain, where the Willow Tit, which gets paler farther north, is very like Marsh Tit in colouring. *Juvs are indistinguishable.* Flight in both typical of tit —fast and flitting. *Marsh Tit has "sst-choo" call,* Willow Tit is subdued for a tit but has buzzing call. Both absent from Ireland and much of Scotland. Neither species has ever been exclusively associated with marsh or willows and either may be found in a variety of woodland, including coppices and wooded gardens. Both species are attracted to bird feeders, localities getting either one species or the other.

Blue Tit

White wing-bar

♂s spread their wings for unusual floating, "butterfly" display flight ◀

All-blue tail

◀ Black eye stripe shows clearly, but central belly streak is always very variable

Blue crown

Alert posture when feeding on ground

Blue Tit is only British sp with all-blue tail. Bold patterns on face and body, and white wing-bar catch eye

♂ in courtship display postures

The commonest tit in the British Isles, a woodland bird that has adapted well to man. It has a small compact crown, which is raised when bird is excited or angry. Flight is fast and undulating with flicking wingbeats — the typical tit flight. Feeds on insects, grubs and caterpillars and is particularly adept at working the flimsy end of branches.

Great Tit

Pale nape patch

Bold markings

Well-marked tail with white outer feathers

Less black on ♀

Pale wing-bar and white cheeks show ▶ in flight

◀ Often feed agilely on nut bags. Note thicker black belly stripe of ♂

Bold black and white head pattern, yellow breast and apple-green back are main pointers

Often feed on ground especially in winter

Largest of the tits and so less acrobatic than the others. Active, inquisitive and quarrelsome, a great visitor to bird tables and user of nest boxes. Juv has brownish crown and yellowish cheeks. Distinctive "tsink-tsink" call, "teecher-teecher-teecher" call in spring and many other calls. Common in woods and gardens throughout British Isles.

Long-tailed Tit

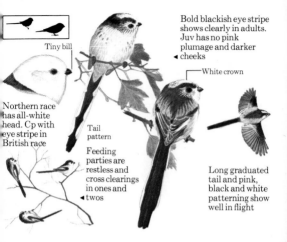

Bold blackish eye stripe shows clearly in adults. Juv has no pink plumage and darker ◄ cheeks

Tiny bill

White crown

Northern race has all-white head. Cp with eye stripe in British race

Tail pattern

Feeding parties are restless and cross clearings in ones and ◄ twos

Long graduated tail and pink, black and white patterning show well in flight

The only *tiny common bird with a long tail*. Apart from its distinctive patterning and tail-waving flight, its constant calls —most often a trilling "tsurup" and a thin "tzee-tzee-tzee"—attract attention. Common throughout British Isles in woodland, scrub, hedges and well-wooded gardens. Severely hit by hard winters; roosts communally for warmth.

Bearded Tit

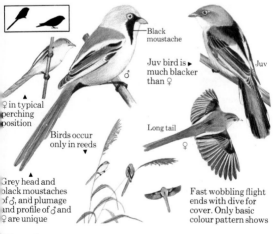

Black moustache

Juv bird is ► much blacker than ♀

Juv

♂

♀ in typical perching position

Birds occur only in reeds ▼

Long tail

Grey head and black moustaches of ♂, and plumage and profile of ♂ and ♀ are unique

♀

Fast wobbling flight ends with dive for cover. Only basic colour pattern shows

Minute size, *tawny colour overall, long tail* and abrupt dives into cover identify this sole European member of babbler family. Feeds on insects in summer and seeds in winter. "Ping" call (like 2 coins flicked together) often betrays their presence. *Rarely, if ever, seen away from Phragmites reeds* and at present breeding sporadically, but increasing in England.

Penduline Tit

Pale bill

Unique "mask"

Entrance

♂ Penduline Tit starts the nest (left), which is built in a tree overhanging water. ♀ helps to finish it.

♂

♀

Maroon band

♀

Grey, black and red of ♂ shows at rest and in flight

No other small European bird has reddish back or maroon band in wing. Lack of throat marks separates from all other tits. Juv has head and back paler than ♀

Very tiny, active bird (smaller than Coal Tit) frequenting trees and vegetation at the edge of rivers, streams, ponds and lakes. Feeds high in tree tops during summer, attracting attention by soft "tsiip-tsiip-tsiip" calls. Forages lower in vegetation during winter. Often occurs in family parties. Spreading into W Europe, but only one record on E coast England

Treecreeper

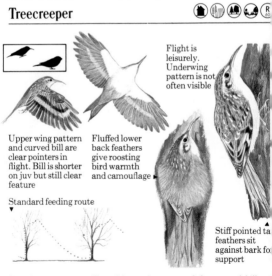

Flight is leisurely. Underwing pattern is not often visible

Upper wing pattern and curved bill are clear pointers in flight. Bill is shorter on juv but still clear feature

Fluffed lower back feathers give roosting bird warmth and camouflage ▶

Standard feeding route
▼

Stiff pointed tail feathers sit against bark for support

Cryptic upperparts, silky white underparts and fine, *curved bill* set Treecreeper apart from all birds. *Tiny and mouse-like in their jerky, spiral movements on tree trunks.* Undulating, unhurried flight. Call, a high, thin "tsee" or "tsit". Common in British Isles. Short-toed species (indistinguishable except by voice) occurs very rarely in SE England.

14

Robin

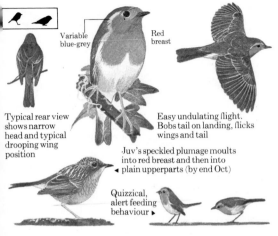

Variable blue-grey

Red breast

Typical rear view shows narrow head and typical drooping wing position

Easy undulating flight. Bobs tail on landing, flicks wings and tail

Juv's speckled plumage moults into red breast and then into ◀ plain upperparts (by end Oct)

Quizzical, alert feeding behaviour ▶

A bold, tame bird, familiar throughout British Isles, yet a shy little-seen woodland bird elsewhere in its range. Highly aggressive, especially in breeding season. Both sexes hold territories in winter. Habit of cocking head, and precise deliberate movement on ground are distinctive. Call, a persistent "tick-tick", also low "tsip". Sings all year round.

Citril Finch

🌳 🦢 Ⓡⓥ

♂'s grey nape yellow-green rump and wing-bars separate it from all other finches

Double wing-bar ♀

Grey

♂

Cp yellower, more heavily streaked Serin ▼

Juv as adults but well streaked and lacks greenish hue ▼

Grey

♀

Long wings (cp Serin and Siskin)

Juv

♀'s wing pattern is less clear than ♂'s

A small sociable finch of high mountain areas, such as the Massif Central and Alps, although occurring at lower altitudes in winter. To be seen in open country as well as conifer woodland. Flocks at end of breeding season. Dancing flight typical of finches. "Tsi-oo" call, also twittering flight call. Has occurred only once in Britain.

Serin

Stubby bill

♂

♀

Yellow rump

♂ has yellow and brown head and yellow breast. ♀ is paler overall with less clear head pattern

Juv is buff overall and heavily streaked with
◄ yellow patch on rump

Yellow breast of ♂ conspicuous, but paler, more streaked in ♀

Smallest of the European finches, with *relatively long wings and short tail*. *Yellow rump* and stubby beak identify and distinguish from Siskin. Swift undulating flight. Tone of twittering flight calls and hard, sharp "zit-zit" draws instant attention. Common on Continent in woodland fringes and urban areas. Has bred in SE England but still uncommon.

Siskin

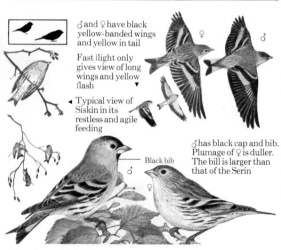

♂ and ♀ have black yellow-banded wings and yellow in tail

Fast flight only gives view of long wings and yellow flash ▼

◄ Typical view of Siskin in its restless and agile feeding

♀

♂

♂ has black cap and bib. Plumage of ♀ is duller. The bill is larger than that of the Serin

Black bib

♂

♀

Tiny, dumpy bird with *forked tail* and *long wings*. *Only small black, green and yellow bird* to occur in British Isles (Serin and Citril Finch are very rare). Call a high clear "tzu" and "tsy-zing". Closely associated with conifers for nesting and with alders and birch in winter. Widely distributed throughout British Isles (especially Scotland).

Redpolls

All Redpolls have same circular, dipping song flight, and also sing from perches and in ordinary flight

Red

♂

Lesser Redpoll

No white (cp Linnet)

Double wing-bars

Pale rump

Mealy Redpoll

Lesser Redpoll

♂ has crimson crown, pink flush on breast, streaky upperparts and pale wing-bars. ♀ lacks pink breast. Black bib on both

Arctic Redpoll

White rump

♂

Arctic Redpoll

Note larger size, paler plumage overall and bold white rump and wing marks

Juv

♂ has pinker breast and is paler overall with more distinct wing-bars than Lesser Redpoll

Lesser Redpoll plumage wears down to dark brown upperparts and almost white underparts by late summer

♂

Mealy Redpoll

Of the 3 Redpoll races, the Arctic of the Far North is the whitest and much the largest, the Mealy, with a northerly distribution, is about two-thirds the Arctic race's size and paler, and the Lesser, of the British Isles and central Europe, is the smallest and darkest. Tiny birds, highly acrobatic in their feeding behaviour. Young birds do not have the red cap and black bib of the adults, but are usually seen with them. Flight active and bounding. Rattling "chi-chi-chi" flight call. Increasing in numbers rapidly and now often seen in wooded gardens. In winter often found with Siskins in waterside alders, and with finches and tits in weed and scrub; in summer frequents conifer and birch.

17

Linnet

Wings and tail of ♂ are blacker, with more white than ♀

Extent of red varies

♂

White

♀

White

♂

Juv resembles ♀ but is more heavily streaked

Juv

Note facial differences ▶ on ♂, ♀ and juv birds

Tiny birds with long wings and tail, short legs and small white area in tail. Tiny black eye and delicate bill are distinctive. Energetic bounding flight. Constant twittering call and song. In winter forms large roving flocks in search of seeds. Common throughout British Isles and may occur in gardens and on roadsides.

Twite

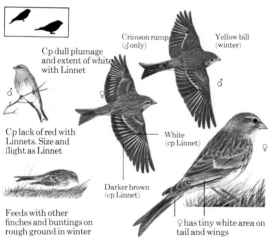

Cp dull plumage and extent of white with Linnet

♂

Crimson rump (♂ only)

Yellow bill (winter)

♂

Cp lack of red with Linnets. Size and flight as Linnet

♀

White (cp Linnet)

♀

Darker brown (cp Linnet)

Feeds with other finches and buntings on rough ground in winter

♀ has tiny white area on tail and wings

Much less common than Linnet. Bill is grey in summer (pale in Linnet); yellow in winter (dark in Linnet). Male and female have less white in wings than Linnet and no obvious white in tail. Twitters constantly in flight. Nasal "twang" call distinct. Occurs only in moorlands: in Britain S to Pennines, and in Ireland (especially in west). Often coastal in winter.

Brambling

♂ has orange shoulders and white wing-bars

♀

Yellow armpit is diagnostic

◀ Summer ♂ has jet-black head and back

♂

Note wing-bars and white rump. Take-off is fast and flight erratic

Note greyish head and pale nape patch ▼

♂

Winter ♀ has ▶ white rump and wing-bars

♂ March

Despite chaffinch-like wing marks, *white rump* sets Brambling apart from all other finches. *Orange, white, black and grey plumage* are further pointers. Much dependent on beech mast, it feeds on the ground and in fields with other finches. Flight call is a rapidly repeated "tchuk-tchuk". Common but erratic winter visitor (Oct–Apr), with odd summer visitors.

Chaffinch

♂

Double wing-bars

♀

◀ White underwing (Cp Brambling)

♀ pattern seen from rear, a ◀ typical view

Black and white on tail

Birds often show peak ◀ on head

Black

♀

♂

♀ and juv are duller but wing pattern is still distinctive

Wing pattern and bright colours of ♂ are distinctive features

Typically seen hopping in series of low, jerky movements with tail down, and often, slight peak on head visible. Feeds on ground singly or in flocks, often with other finches. *Extremely undulating flight* shows green rump and white wing-bars. Loud "chink-chink" call with "chip" flight call. Commonest of British finches with large Continental influx in October.

Goldfinch

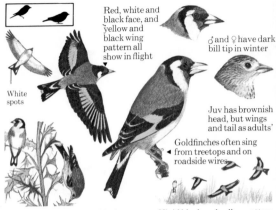

Red, white and black face, and yellow and black wing pattern all show in flight

♂ and ♀ have dark bill tip in winter

White spots

Juv has brownish head, but wings and tail as adults'

Goldfinches often sing from treetops and on roadside wires

Typical view of birds on thistle. They often feed head down

Vivid black and yellow pattern and bouncing flight are unique

A bird of woodland fringes, scrub and waste ground, found wherever there are thistles and weeds, from which its long, sharp bill extracts the seeds. *Fluent liquid, twittering "switt-switt-switt" call.* Song an elaboration of this call. Common throughout British Isles, but absent from N Scotland. Part of population migrates south in winter.

Greenfinch

♂

Only ♂ has grey in wings. Note yellow and black

Yellow wing panel

♀ is browner above and not as bright as ♂

Display

Black and yellow

Juv

Flight very undulating. ♂ has "butterfly" display flight over trees

Juv is streaked. Cp ♀ sparrow but note wing panel

Heavy, muscular finch with a strong bill, long wings and a short, forked tail. *Overall greenish hue* all year and colours especially brilliant in spring. Aggressive and quarrelsome, particularly at bird tables. Flocks in fields with other finches in winter. Call a rapid, *harsh trill* and drawn-out, *nasal "sweee".* Common throughout British Isles.

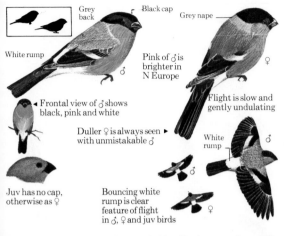

Grey back

Black cap

Grey nape

White rump

Pink of ♂ is brighter in N Europe

♀

◄ Frontal view of ♂ shows black, pink and white

Duller ♀ is always seen ► with unmistakable ♂

Flight is slow and gently undulating

White rump

♂

Juv has no cap, otherwise as ♀

Bouncing white rump is clear feature of flight in ♂, ♀ and juv birds

♀

Retiring bird, but bright colours make identification easy. Stout bill follows head line in almost continuous curve. Usually feeds in trees on woodland fringe, but also common in hedges and gardens. Eats buds in spring and also picks seeds on ground. Located by distinct, *soft "pheeu"* call. Young have squealing call. Common throughout British Isles.

Hawfinch

Grey nape

Huge bill

Juv

Pale tip

White wing-bars

White wing panel

Bill is bluish in summer and horn-coloured in winter. Wing and tail marks show on take-off, and ◄ on underwing in flight

Juv lacks adult head pattern, and has crescentic bars below

The largest finch, with *huge bill*, long wings and *short square tail*. From a distance bill and *grey nape* show well. Extremely shy and wary. Progresses by very long hops along ground. Flight strong and undulating, often high. Loud explosive "tick" call is best means of location. Woodland bird that visits large gardens. Occurs S of Aberdeen.

Crossbills

"Gyp-gyp" call attracts attention to flying birds ♂

Grey-green upperparts, yellowish underparts and rump identify ♀

♀

♀

♂ is brick-red, esp on rump. ♂, ♀ and juv have dark wings and tail

Bill is not crossed in fledglings

Common

Scottish Crossbill

Parrot

◄ Typical view of Crossbill feeding. Very long wings with short forked tail stand out

Upper mandible is straight, lower crosses it laterally

Crossbills are well adapted to eating pine seeds. Parrot Crossbill has the heaviest bill and deeper call also identifies it

Juv is greenish yellow and very heavily streaked on head, back and breast

Birds descend to drink at puddles or feed on fallen cones

Unique crossed bill, used for prising seeds from pine cones, is unmistakable close to. From a distance, long wings, short tail and *parrot-like clambering over branches* are distinctive. Plumage varies greatly as birds mature, from yellows and greens through orange to the bright red of adult male. Bill size also varies; birds feeding on Scots pine in Britain have larger bills than those feeding on spruce on the Continent. Entirely confined to conifers, breeding mainly in mature plantations. Nests early Dec onwards, but mostly Feb-Apr. Patchy, local distribution throughout Britain. Occurs rarely in Ireland. Subject to periodic irruptions from the Continent in lean food years, and also wanders out of breeding areas.

Wood and Marshland Birds

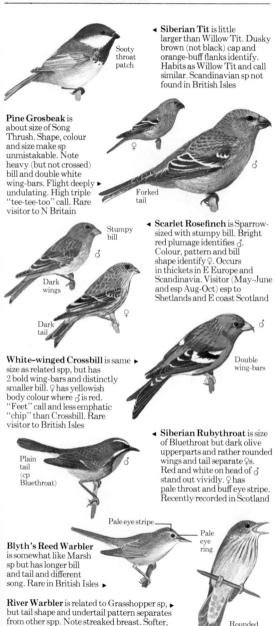

Sooty throat patch

◄ **Siberian Tit** is little larger than Willow Tit. Dusky brown (not black) cap and orange-buff flanks identify. Habits as Willow Tit and call similar. Scandinavian sp not found in British Isles

Pine Grosbeak is about size of Song Thrush. Shape, colour and size make sp unmistakable. Note heavy (but not crossed) bill and double white wing-bars. Flight deeply ► undulating. High triple "tee-tee-too" call. Rare visitor to N Britain

♀

♂

Forked tail

Stumpy bill

♂

Dark wings

Dark tail

♀

◄ **Scarlet Rosefinch** is Sparrow-sized with stumpy bill. Bright red plumage identifies ♂. Colour, pattern and bill shape identify ♀. Occurs in thickets in E Europe and Scandinavia. Visitor (May-June and esp Aug-Oct) esp to Shetlands and E coast Scotland

White-winged Crossbill is same ► size as related spp, but has 2 bold wing-bars and distinctly smaller bill. ♀ has yellowish body colour where ♂ is red. "Feet" call and less emphatic "chip" than Crossbill. Rare visitor to British Isles

♂

Double wing-bars

Plain tail (cp Bluethroat)

♂

◄ **Siberian Rubythroat** is size of Bluethroat but dark olive upperparts and rather rounded wings and tail separate ♀s. Red and white on head of ♂ stand out vividly. ♀ has pale throat and buff eye stripe. Recently recorded in Scotland

Pale eye stripe

Pale eye ring

Blyth's Reed Warbler is somewhat like Marsh sp but has longer bill and tail and different song. Rare in British Isles ►

River Warbler is related to Grasshopper sp, ► but tail shape and undertail pattern separates from other spp. Note streaked breast. Softer, slower song than Grasshopper. Rare in British Isles

Rounded tail

23

Great Reed Warbler

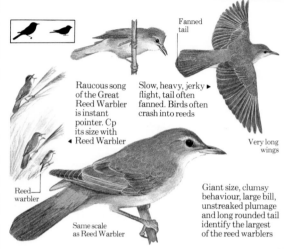

Raucous song of the Great Reed Warbler is instant pointer. Cp its size with ◄ Reed Warbler

Fanned tail

Slow, heavy, jerky ► flight, tail often fanned. Birds often crash into reeds

Very long wings

Reed warbler

Same scale as Reed Warbler

Giant size, clumsy behaviour, large bill, unstreaked plumage and long rounded tail identify the largest of the reed warblers

Much the *largest of the reed warblers*. General shape and plumage resembles the Reed Warbler, but features, particularly bill, are heavier. *Clumsy movements* and strident, grating "kara-kara-brik-brik-gurk-gurk" song will attract attention. Confined to marshy areas. Occurs very rarely May–Sept in Britain but may yet colonize.

Savi's Warbler

Pale eye stripe

Tail-cocking ► action is not seen in Reed Warbler. Swift, low flight over reeds. Sharp "spitz" call will identify bird

◄ Pale breast, buff underparts differ from Reed Warbler. Curved stubby wings and body shape also set them apart

Long buff undertail coverts

Nest is built on ► reed base

Broadly resembles Reed Warbler but is actually related to Grasshopper Warbler. *Only unstreaked warbler with buzzing song.* Large for a warbler and stubby, with short wings and ample, well-rounded tail. Song is very like Grasshopper Warbler's but lower in pitch. Rare in Britain but now recolonizing East Anglia, and in S of England

Singing birds relax, looking fatter than in ◀ other postures

The Reed Warbler's bounding, jerky flight is identical to that of Marsh Warbler ▶

Reed Warbler

Pale eye ring

◀ Juv shows slightly paler throat and more rufous underparts than adults

Reed Warbler

Paler in front of eye

Both spp are very alike and juvs are extremely hard to distinguish. Marsh Warbler has marginally longer wing tips and has uniformly pale underparts which show little tonal variation. Note also its pale legs against the grey-brown of Reed Warbler's legs

Marsh Warbler

Longer wing tip of Marsh Warbler

Eye ring whiter in Marsh Warbler

Reed Warbler

◀ Both species are adept at moving in thick growth. Reed Warblers often adopt vertical head-down posture

Marsh Warbler

Nest of Marsh Warbler is bound to surrounding stems. Reed's deep cup is built into reed stems

Marsh Warbler

Reed and Marsh Warblers are slim, sharp-faced, active birds of sober coloration. Extremely difficult to tell apart, but Marsh Warbler's plumage is colder coloured, and its unrelieved, plainer markings both above and below give a notably neater appearance. Marsh Warbler's general deportment is more horizontal. Reed Warbler is usually confined to reed beds and their borders, whereas Marsh Warbler is found in low vegetation including osiers. Nests are quite different. *Marsh Warbler's song far more melodious than Reed's* harsh, chattering jumble of "churrur-churrur" and "jag-jag-jag" notes. Reed Warbler breeds S of Ripon. Marsh Warbler only in about 20 localities in southern half of England and Wales.

Aquatic Warbler

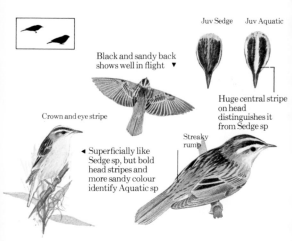

Juv Sedge   Juv Aquatic

Black and sandy back
shows well in flight ▼

Huge central stripe
on head
distinguishes it
from Sedge sp

Crown and eye stripe

Streaky
rump

◄ Superficially like
Sedge sp, but bold
head stripes and
more sandy colour
identify Aquatic sp

Same size as Sedge Warbler but much more skulking. At close quarters all feathers, especially tail, look very pointed. Juvenile bird may be confused with young Sedge Warbler, which shows a faint central head stripe. Call as Sedge Warbler. Regular visitor to British Isles mainly to S England, Aug-Oct, but also a few birds occur in spring.

Sedge Warbler

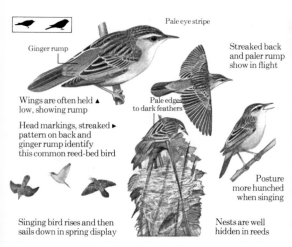

Pale eye stripe

Ginger rump

Streaked back
and paler rump
show in flight

Wings are often held ▲
low, showing rump

Pale edges
to dark feathers

Head markings, streaked ►
pattern on back and
ginger rump identify
this common reed-bed bird

Posture
more hunched
when singing

Singing bird rises and then
sails down in spring display

Nests are well
hidden in reeds

Active, rather ebullient bird but with some of the skulking habits of other reed-bed warblers. Often emerges from low vegetation to sing noisily. May look slim or quite stocky. Flies low, often with depressed tail, usually for short distance. Hard "tuck" alarm call. Found both in reeds and vegetation around wet areas. Widely distributed Apr-Sept in British Isles.

Cetti's Warbler

White eye stripe

Ragged-looking
rounded tail

Dark, rich brown plumage
above grey breast and
long, rounded tail make
identification easy

◄ Usually skulks low in
scrub, but occasionally
emerges into full view
with intermittent upward
flicks of tail

Rounded wing, long tail ►
and dark coloration
identify bird in flight

More robustly built than other marshland warblers. Its flight is low and
fairly rapid. Typical warbler churring alarm call, or more emphatic single
"chic". *Song is loud and explosive*, usually erupting from low vegetation.
Occurs in wet areas and nearby ditches and hedges. Recent arrival,
confined to extreme SE England but now spreading.

Grasshopper Warbler

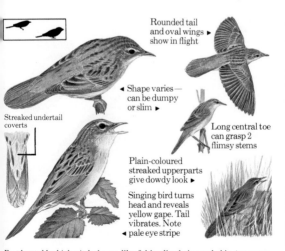

Rounded tail
and oval wings ►
show in flight

◄ Shape varies —
can be dumpy
or slim ►

Streaked undertail
coverts

Long central toe
can grasp 2
flimsy stems

Plain-coloured
streaked upperparts
give dowdy look ►

Singing bird turns
head and reveals
yellow gape. Tail
vibrates. Note
◄ pale eye stripe

Best located by high-pitched song, like fishing line being reeled in (compare
Savi's Warbler). A shy bird, adept at moving in thick vegetation and
hiding in the scantest cover, it is usually only seen when singing. Occurs in
any rank grass, heath or in forestry plantations. Population fluctuates, but
widespread Apr-Sept.

Nightingale

♂ in display fans
wings and tail. Note
orange-brown under-
tail and white belly

Singing with
tail cocked
(a common habit)
and crown raised ►

Pale throat
and underparts

Juv as adult but has
"scaly" look to breast
and upperparts

Adult at nest deep
in vegetation. Birds
accost intruders with
deep scolding call and
wing and tail flicking

A shy, skulking bird keeping to thick vegetation in damp woods, copses and hedges. Plump and well built with *rich, rufous-brown upperparts and long, rounded tail* very evident in flight. Famous song, heard by day and night, is a slow "pieu-pieu-pieu", then explosive "chock-chock-chock" and great crescendo. Breeds in England S of Humber and Dee (Apr-Sept).

Thrush Nightingale

Same size and shape
as Nightingale but
has more olive upper-
parts. Tail is less
rufous but colour is
visible nevertheless

Nightingale spp
closely resemble each
other but dark throat
streaks identify
Thrush Nightingale ►

◄ Frontal view shows
spotted breast and
prominent pale
throat patch

Cp tail of
Nightingale

Juv has wings and tail as ►
adults but head, back and
breast are heavily spotted

Resembles Nightingale in shape, size and behaviour. Pale area on throat is divided by darker line on either side. Breast is well marked and belly pale. Undertail is dull orange with undertail coverts creamy. Song is as melodious as the Nightingale's, but it lacks a crescendo. Occupies similar habitat but prefers damper localities. Very rare in Britain (May-Oct).

Garden Warbler

Garden Warbler is ▶ usually seen flitting from bush to bush

Juv's underparts have a yellowish cast

Shortish tail (cp Blackcap)

Rounded head, bill relatively short for a warbler and rather blank look are distinctive

Subtle grey patch

Pale eye stripe

Large dark eye and pale eye ring

Juv

Superficially nondescript bird of woodland and scrub. Song is a pleasant warble very like Blackcap's. Habitat overlaps with Blackcap, but Garden Warbler occupies more open areas and is absent from wooded urban areas. Fairly well distributed mid Apr-Oct in England, Wales and E Scotland. Uncommon in Ireland.

Blackcap

♂

♂

Grey nape

♂s sing deep in foliage

Tail stands out in swift, jerky flight

Brown cap

Black cap, grey nape and breast, olive-brown upperparts in ♂. ♀ has brownish tinge on grey breast

♀

Rufous-brown cap

♀

Juv

A slim, elegant bird with longish wings and tail. Active and lively, but usually hugs the cover of woodland trees and bushes. Song is rich and melodious in contrast with "tack-tack" alarm call and confusable with that of Garden Warbler. Found in open woodland and large wooded gardens, in England and Wales. Sporadic in Scotland and Ireland.

Wood Warbler

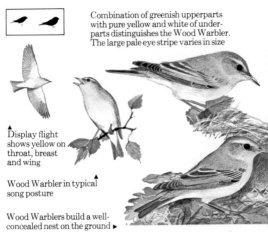

Combination of greenish upperparts with pure yellow and white of underparts distinguishes the Wood Warbler. The large pale eye stripe varies in size

Display flight shows yellow on throat, breast and wing

Wood Warbler in typical song posture

Wood Warblers build a well-concealed nest on the ground ►

Largest greenish-plumaged warbler to breed in British Isles. Slim, elegant bird with long wings and short tail. Makes frequent sallies after insects and will hover. Has sailing, gliding display flight. Song is a shivering trill. Found Apr-Sept in woodland with a good canopy and little ground cover. Extremely rare on passage in Britain and very rare at any time in Ireland.

Bonelli's Warbler

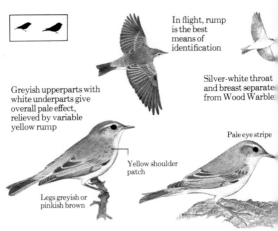

In flight, rump is the best means of identification

Silver-white throat and breast separate from Wood Warbler

Greyish upperparts with white underparts give overall pale effect, relieved by variable yellow rump

Pale eye stripe

Yellow shoulder patch

Legs greyish or pinkish brown

Smaller than the very similar Wood Warbler, Bonelli's Warbler is a long-winged, delicately built bird. Song is a rather slow, short trill on a single note with a "too-weet" call more emphatic than that of the similar-looking but much commoner Willow Warbler. Rare visitor to Britain Apr-Oct (especially Sept).

Icterine Warbler

Orange cutting edges

Long broad-based bill

Pale wing panel

Long protruding wing tip

Large and heavily built for a warbler, with long wings noticeable both in flight and at rest

Singing ♂ often raises crown ►

Orange gape

Very yellow underparts

Juv

Long wings and tail (cp Melodious)

Feeding birds tug berries off in a unique way

Much less dainty than the typical warbler, the Icterine Warbler is an active, lively bird to be found in the trees of woods, parks and gardens. Yellow in adults fades to brownish shade by autumn. *Legs are bluish-grey.* Flight less hurried than in other warblers, and similar to Spotted Flycatcher's. Scarce passage migrant.

Melodious Warbler

Pale eye stripe

Yellower (cp adult)

Shorter tail and wings (cp Icterine)

Juv ▲

Long, broad beak is similar to Icterine's but head of Melodious is flatter

Towards autumn, adult ► plumage can get very worn, but heavy head and dumpy shape overall are still distinctive

Autumn

Large, heavy bird very like the Icterine Warbler but with a musical song. Two species are never found together, Melodious occurring in thick bushes and high scrub. Can be seen when singing but generally very shy. Legs are less blue than Icterine's. Has a parachute display flight similar to Tree Pipit. Very rare passage migrant.

Willow Warbler

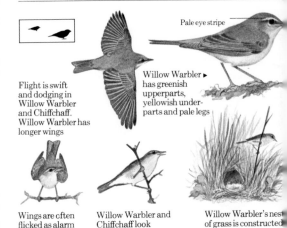

Pale eye stripe

Willow Warbler ▶
has greenish
upperparts,
yellowish under-
parts and pale legs

Flight is swift
and dodging in
Willow Warbler
and Chiffchaff.
Willow Warbler has
longer wings

Wings are often
flicked as alarm
call is given

Willow Warbler and
Chiffchaff look
alike from below

Willow Warbler's nest
of grass is constructed
on the ground

A bird of similar habits and appearance to the Chiffchaff. Both catch flies by flitting, chasing sallies, or by hovering. Willow Warbler is a bird of small bushes and young trees and vegetation, but both species will feed high in trees or in low bushes, especially on passage. Most numerous summer migrant (Apr-Oct) in British Isles.

Chiffchaff

◀ Chiffchaff has a
rounder head, shorter
wing tips and, usually
darker legs than the
Willow Warbler

Juv is much yellower
than adult, which has
almost buff underparts
and brownish upperparts

Shorter wing-tip
(cp Willow Warbler)

Chiffchaff nest is a
ragged domed structure
built above ground ▶

Typical singing and perching postures.
Birds slip quietly through foliage, picking
at food, or take flight to catch insects

A small, delicate warbler with slight physical differences to Willow Warbler, but otherwise identical. Song, however, is absolutely distinctive, a *deliberate "teet-teu"* often repeated. Shares a *low, anxious "houeet" call* with Willow Warbler. Found in woodland and scrub throughout British Isles Mar-Oct, but some overwinter.

Arctic Warbler

Yellow-white eye stripe

Bill brown above and orangish-yellow below

Faint wing-bar (not always present)

Very long eye stripe, flatter head shape and longer, less compact build distinguish from Willow Warbler

Wing-bar (may wear off or show more on one side)

Pale legs (sometimes greyish)

Willow Warbler

Juv is darker green above and yellower below than adult, with pale brown or flesh-coloured bill

Similar-looking Willow Warbler has long wing tips

Larger size, distinctive facial appearance and pale wing-bar or bars distinguish it from Willow Warbler. Typical warbler flight. Song is a shivering, repeated "ziz-ziz-zy-zy" followed by short whistle. Call, rough "tiwee-ip" and more emphatic "chick". Scarce migrant Aug-Oct, especially to Fair Isle, but also scattered around rest of British Isles.

Greenish Warbler

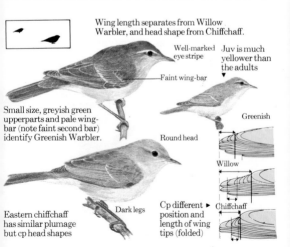

Wing length separates from Willow Warbler, and head shape from Chiffchaff.

Well-marked eye stripe

Juv is much yellower than the adults

Faint wing-bar

Small size, greyish green upperparts and pale wing-bar (note faint second bar) identify Greenish Warbler.

Greenish

Round head

Willow

Eastern chiffchaff has similar plumage but cp head shapes

Dark legs

Cp different position and length of wing tips (folded)

Chiffchaff

Greatly resembles the Chiffchaff but has a flatter forehead. Adult plumage is very worn when it arrives on autumn passage (may be seen with Chiffchaffs and Willow Warblers then). Chiffchaff-like flight. Diagnostic "see-ee" call. Expanding into NW Europe. About 5 occur annually, Aug-Dec, in British Isles and numbers are increasing.

Whitethroat

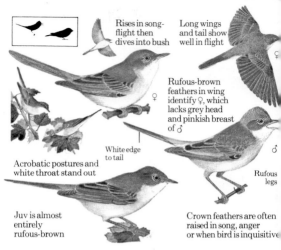

Rises in song-flight then dives into bush

Long wings and tail show well in flight

♀

Rufous-brown feathers in wing identify ♀, which lacks grey head and pinkish breast of ♂

♂

White edge to tail

Rufous legs

Acrobatic postures and white throat stand out

Juv is almost entirely rufous-brown

Crown feathers are often raised in song, anger or when bird is inquisitive

Lanky, restless, nervously energetic bird with *long tail and expressive face*. Male's display flight involves rocketing climbs and plummeting dives into cover. Flight over a distance is undulating. Dives into cover of hedges and scrub after brief evasion flight and scolds intruder from cover. Scratchy pleasant song. Summer visitor (Apr-Oct), much decreased since 1968.

Lesser Whitethroat

◀ Juv has pure grey head plumage and dark ear coverts

♀

Legs bluish grey (cp Whitethroat)

White edge to tail

Looks shorter in tail, smaller and greyer than Whitethroat

◀ Forages quietly for insects in tree foliage

♂

White throat

♀

♀ looks pale greyish. All birds have pale wing panel

Spring ♂ has grey head, variable, sometimes pink flushed breast. No rufous in wings (cp Whitethroat

Smaller, shorter-tailed bird than closely related Whitethroat. Also distinctly greyer in tone but with buff wing edges. *Often looks very pale against background of its tall hedge and scrub habitat.* Fairly secretive unlike brasher Whitethroat. Call a distinctive rattle. Summer visitor (mid Apr-Oct). Widespread in England and Wales, sparse in Scotland.

34

Sardinian Warbler

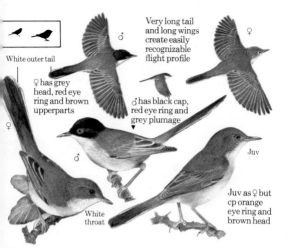

Very long tail and long wings create easily recognizable flight profile

♂

♀

White outer tail

♀ has grey head, red eye ring and brown upperparts

♂ has black cap, red eye ring and grey plumage ▼

♂

White throat

Juv

Juv as ♀ but cp orange eye ring and brown head

Lively, noisy birds of inquisitive disposition. Normally skulking and difficult to catch sight of, but can be very tame. Deliberate wingbeats of birds flying into tree are striking. Harsh, *fast, stuttering "stititic" call* is a familiar feature of the Mediterranean scrubland which it inhabits. Very rare vagrant to British Isles.

Subalpine Warbler

Juv

Tiny size and ► blue-grey upperparts identify ♂ in flight

♂

Juv has white undertail coverts and gold eye ring ▼

Juv

◄ Buff in juv's wing and throat separates from Whitethroat

Buff colour in ♀ and juv

Red eye ring

♂

♀ has red eye ring and pinkish underparts

♀ Grey upperparts, white moustache and pink upperparts of ♂ are unique

Tiny, delicate birds with fairly long tails. Males are easy to identify, but there are considerable variations in female plumage, which can be very pink below (average plumage is shown). Juvenile is confusable with Whitethroat. Sharp "teck-teck" call. A shy bird of Mediterranean scrubland and only a rare vagrant in the British Isles.

Dartford Warbler

Looks dark in flight

◄ Tail is carried high in weak, bounding flight

Dartford Warbler's cocked tail is about half its body length

♀ feeding paler-breasted juv. Short-tailed when they emerge from nest, juvs grow to full size in about 10 days ▼

♀

Crown often raised

Red eye and rim

♂

Speckled white on often distended throat

Short tail of juv

Tiny size, long tail, stubby wings and dark coloration are unique. Formerly widespread but now *confined to gorse and heath* in extreme S England. Lively, active insect eaters. Regarded as secretive but soft, buzzy "gee-ee-ip" calls betray presence. Hard winters had reduced population to 10 pairs only, but now recovering and standing at about 600 pairs.

Fan-tailed Warbler

Wren-like profile in flight

Has "zip-zip" call and energetic, jerky climb in display flight

Tiny size, stubby wings and rounded tail are distinctive

Typical rear view

Stocky build, alert posture and tail-cocking are distinctive

Underside of tail

Upperparts well ► marked, rufous rump, beady eye and longish bill are distinctive

Only member of its widespread family to occur in Europe. Shape, size and vociferous "zip" and "teu" calls are unmistakable. Occurring in a wide variety of vegetation in marsh or dry ground with ditches, but seldom seen unless perched on wires or glimpsed in flight. Rare in British Isles but moving north in Europe and may well colonize England.

Stonechat

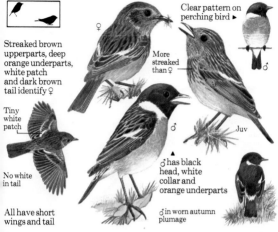

Clear pattern on perching bird ▶

Streaked brown
upperparts, deep
orange underparts,
white patch
and dark brown
tail identify ♀

More
streaked
than ♀

♂

Tiny
white
patch

Juv

No white
in tail

♂ has black
head, white
collar and
orange underparts

All have short
wings and tail

♂ in worn autumn
plumage

Tiny size, more dumpy profile, short wings and dark, short tail distinguish
Stonechat from Whinchat. Easily missed in its heath and moorland
habitat, but perches prominently on bushes, wires and fences. Constantly
flirts its tail and flicks its wings. Flight somewhat whirring. Call a constant
"tak-tak". Single birds winter out of breeding area in rough ground.

Whinchat

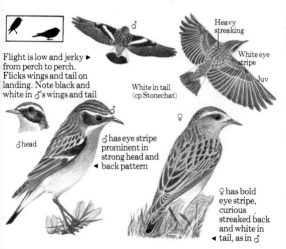

♂

Heavy
streaking

Flight is low and jerky ▶
from perch to perch.
Flicks wings and tail on
landing. Note black and
white in ♂'s wings and tail

White eye
stripe

Juv

White in tail
(cp Stonechat)

♂ head

♂

♂ has eye stripe
prominent in
strong head and
back pattern ◀

♀

♀ has bold
eye stripe,
curious
streaked back
and white in
tail, as in ♂ ◀

Striking small bird of heath and rough grass with perches (includes young
forestry plantations) often confused with Stonechat. At all times, *white in
Whinchat's tail distinguishes from Stonechat*. Erect posture and constant
flicking tail and wings are distinctive. Call is a harsh "tik-tik", with brief,
simple song. Summer visitor (Apr-Oct). Throughout British Isles.

37

Wheatear

Buff upperparts

Typical view of Wheatear in flight showing white rump and black tail band

Juv

♂

♀

Juv autumn plumage

◀ Greenland race

Juv autumn plumage

Juv autumn plumage

Black legs (all birds)

♂ spring

Greenland Wheatear is larger, longer winged with brighter plumage

♂ July

◀ Spring ♂ has grey crown and back contrasting with black face patch, wings and tail. Worn feathers make plumage contrast stronger

Wear dulls the bright colours of autumn. Cp variety of poses birds adopt

Adult ♂ has grey crown and back

Juv has rich buff back and
◀ rufous in wings

♀ in spring plumage

Despite wide variation in plumage between individual adults, *white and black in tail make the Wheatear instantly identifiable*. Erect posture, active disposition and dapper appearance are also distinctive. Constant bowing and bobbing, with flicking and wagging of short tail are characteristic, interspersed with quick scurries to perch on a vantage point. Flight is low and dashing from perch to perch. Flies after insects or runs short distances to pick food off ground. Bolts for cover into holes. Hole nester. Among earliest of spring arrivals. Distributed throughout British Isles (early Mar-late Oct), but local in S England and much commoner north of line from Severn to Humber.

Bluethroat

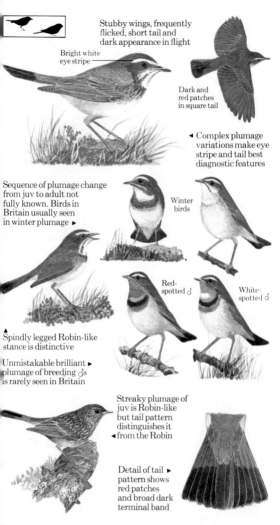

Stubby wings, frequently flicked, short tail and dark appearance in flight

Bright white eye stripe

Dark and red patches in square tail

◄ Complex plumage variations make eye stripe and tail best diagnostic features

Sequence of plumage change from juv to adult not fully known. Birds in Britain usually seen in winter plumage ►

Winter birds

Red-spotted ♂

White-spotted ♂

▲ Spindly legged Robin-like stance is distinctive

Unmistakable brilliant ► plumage of breeding ♂s is rarely seen in Britain

Streaky plumage of juv is Robin-like but tail pattern distinguishes it ◄ from the Robin

Detail of tail ► pattern shows red patches and broad dark terminal band

Extremely shy bird, largely keeps to the cover of its low vegetation habitat. Breeding birds more visible and passage migrants may be seen in seaside bushes. If flushed, flies low, thrusting into cover at ground level, but may emerge into open again to feed. Has a "tack-tack" call. Western European breeding birds (ranging as far south as central S France) are white spotted. Birds breeding in Scandinavia are red spotted. Mainly autumn passage migrant (Aug-Oct), especially Scottish islands and E coast of Scotland and England. Formerly scarce in British Isles, but now increasingly to be seen in Scotland in the spring and has attempted to nest once (in 1968).

Black Redstart

White
Broader wing
(cp Redstart)

♀

Winter ♂ replaces
◄ black upperparts
with sooty grey

Summer ♂ has jet ►
black body and
white wing panel

Sooty brown ♀ ►
lacks Redstart's
eye ring and
pale throat

♂

♀

Orange
tail

Larger than Redstart yet easily overlooked. Similar in behaviour, including distinctive *tail shivering,* but spends more time ground feeding. Nests in city buildings (especially power stations), ruins and rock faces. Tending to be single in winter. *Distinctive song like jangling keys.* Breeds S England with some single winter and passage birds. Well known on Continent.

Barred Warbler

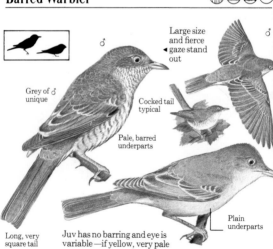

Large size
and fierce
◄ gaze stand
out

♂

♂

Grey of ♂
unique

Cocked tail
typical

Pale, barred
underparts

Plain
underparts

Long, very
square tail

Juv has no barring and eye is
variable —if yellow, very pale

Fierce facial expression, and pattern and colour of plumage identify this robust warbler. Females browner and less distinctly barred than males. Eye in male can vary in intensity of colour. Raises crown and jerks tail when excited. Heavy, rather jerky flight. "Chack-chack" call from cover, also churring note. Passage migrant to E coast of Britain (Sept-Oct).

White forehead, black mask

Orange-red tail and rump of ♀, together with warm buff upperparts, distinguishes from larger Black Redstart ▶

Orange-red tail and rump and pale grey upperparts, together with absence of white in wing, distinguishes ♂ from Black Redstart ▲

◀ Adult ♀ and imm are pale grey-buff above with dark eye set in pale eye ring, and pale throat, separating them at once from Black Redstart

♀

Imm ♂s have blackish face edged in white, buff crown and browner upperparts than fully mature adult. Underparts are paler ▶

imm ♂

Pale throat (♀ and juv)

♀

Black throat

Juv has crescent markings on underparts and is much lighter overall than young Black Redstarts

♂

Unmistakable black and red ♂ in breeding plumage

Slim, delicate birds always seen in or near trees or perched on walls or wire fences. Makes constantly repeated sallies after insects. *Tail is bobbed and constantly "shivered"*. Fluttering, hovering flight after insects and elegant glides on its long wings before landing. "Houeet" alarm call (not unlike Willow Warbler) and a soft "whit-ti-tik" contact call. Prefers deciduous woods (open canopy and undergrowth) and also occurs in parks, gardens and areas of scattered trees. Nests in holes in trees or stone walls and will use nest boxes. Males arrive first in mid-Apr, all birds departing Oct. Often seen on coast Aug-Oct on passage. Widely distributed in Britain, but occurs only rarely in Ireland.

Pied Flycatcher

Black and white breeding plumage fades at end of nesting season

Adult ♂ summer

Pure white underparts

White wing-bars

Imm birds are as ♀ but have buff not white edges to wings. All birds wag tail constantly ►

White

Longish wings, large dark eye and tiny legs are distinctive in the Pied Flycatcher. The male in autumn is like the female. Sits quietly on wall or in foliage and then makes flitting, gliding flights after insects. Call, a quiet "tik-tik" typical of flycatchers. Found in deciduous woodlands W of line from Humber to Portland Bill (mid Apr-Oct).

Collared Flycatcher

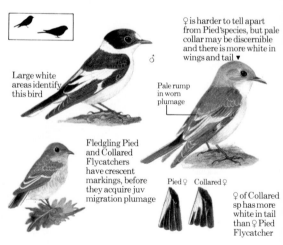

♀ is harder to tell apart from Pied species, but pale collar may be discernible and there is more white in wings and tail ▼

Large white areas identify this bird

♂

Pale rump in worn plumage

Fledgling Pied and Collared Flycatchers have crescent markings, before they acquire juv migration plumage

Pied ♀   Collared ♀

♀ of Collared sp has more white in tail than ♀ Pied Flycatcher

Similar appearance and habits make distinction from the Pied Flycatcher difficult except when male is in breeding plumage. Female has only subtlest distinction from Pied species and plumage variations in each may render them indistinguishable. Very rare vagrant from S and E Europe. At most one every two or three years.

Spotted Flycatcher

Large, dark eye in pale head

Note spotted plumage of juv

Long wings aid effortless, aerobatic flight

Flat bill
Faint streaks

Look for quiet, greyish bird, often slowly wagging tail ▶

Often seen drooping and flicking wings

◀ Adults are streaked, not spotted. Note short black legs

Long-winged, sparrow-sized bird, with brown upperparts and otherwise non-descript plumage. Quiet watching from a tree perch is interspersed with aerobatic sallies after insects, and tortuous flight just off ground. Call is a high "tsit" or "tsit-tuk-tuk". Found throughout the British Isles (late May-Sept).

Red-breasted Flycatcher

Red breast of ♂ is unique among the flycatchers and not even confusable with the larger Robin. Grey head of ♂ only is also ◀ a diagnostic feature

Flight is typical of flycatchers but white flashes on the tail (cp tail of much larger Wheatear) distinguish it from all other spp

Tail (above)

◀ ♀ and juv lack grey head and orange breast, but tiny size, shape, pale eye ring, and tail cocking and flycatching behaviour make them unmistakable

Juv

Smallest of the flycatchers. Despite its apparently conspicuous colours, can be very retiring and is often overlooked in its thick woodland habitat. Makes typical brief, slightly undulating sorties after insects. "Chic", and Wren-like ticking calls. A regular passage migrant to British Isles, especially E and S coast. Occurs rarely in spring.

Yellowhammer

Spring ♂s head ▶ is beacon-like

Rufous rump distinguishes bird from other buntings. Tail is constantly flicked

Yellow underparts and armpit

Yellow head

♂

Streaked breast

Juv

Variable russet breast

♂

Birds look slim and long-tailed when feeding

♀

Rufous

White

Common bird of fields, hedges and open gardens throughout British Isles. Usually seen in pairs. In winter forms feeding flocks with other species and may be seen feeding at roadside. Noticeably long winged and long tailed in flight. Sings a monotonous rattle ending in a flourish from perch on wires. Ringing "tink" flight call.

Ortolan

In flight birds look long and slim

♂

♀ has duller head colouring

♂

Adults have pink ▶ bill, and unique facial expression

♂

Square tail (cp Yellowhammer)

◀ Note breast pattern of ♂

◀ Juv has white eye ring, yellowish tinge below and same look as adult

Noticeably slim even for a bunting. *Greenish head, pale eye ring, yellow throat and orange underparts of male* are unique. Eye and bill give *unmistakable facial expression*. Rump in all ages is golden-buff. Rather clipped "tlip" flight call. Widely distributed in Europe, but occurs in Britain only as an occasional passage migrant, mainly Aug-Oct.

Cirl Bunting

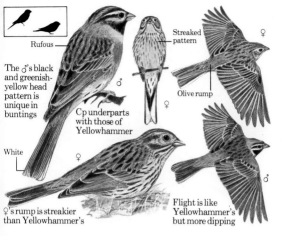

Rufous

The ♂'s black and greenish-yellow head pattern is unique in buntings

Streaked pattern

♀

Olive rump

Cp underparts with those of Yellowhammer

White

♀

♀'s rump is streakier than Yellowhammer's

Flight is like Yellowhammer's but more dipping

♂

Easily overlooked bird; female and juvenile in particular confusable with Yellowhammer, but *olive rump on all birds* distinguishes. Call is a thin "zit" or "sip" and its rattling song is not unlike Lesser Whitethroat's. Restricted to England (Worcester area and line S of Gloucester-Luton) and now declining. Associated with elms.

Rock Bunting

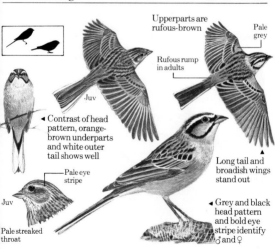

Upperparts are rufous-brown

Pale grey

Rufous rump in adults

Juv

Contrast of head pattern, orange-brown underparts and white outer tail shows well

Pale eye stripe

Juv

Pale streaked throat

Long tail and broadish wings stand out

Grey and black head pattern and bold eye stripe identify ♂ and ♀

Typical long-tailed bunting, common on rocky hillsides and roads, very like Yellowhammer in habits – wary and quick to take flight. *Only juvs are difficult to identify but have inner wing and upper tail rufous* and buff underparts. These, contrasting with eye stripe and throat, are diagnostic. Undulating flight. Very rare vagrant to England and Wales.

Reed Bunting

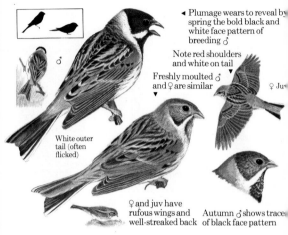

◄ Plumage wears to reveal by spring the bold black and white face pattern of breeding ♂

Note red shoulders and white on tail ▼

Freshly moulted ♂ and ♀ are similar ▼

♀ Juv

♂

White outer tail (often flicked)

♀ and juv have rufous wings and well-streaked back

Autumn ♂ shows traces of black face pattern

An active, conspicuous bird which usually perches prominently yet is easily overlooked when creeping over ground for food. Flight undulating and erratic, and only over short distances. "Seep" contact call, and metallic "chink" and *irritating, tinkling song*. Habitat now includes drier as well as marshy areas. Common throughout British Isles.

Lapland Bunting

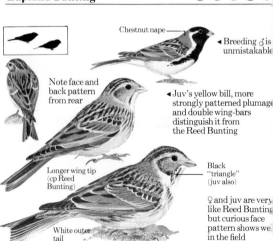

Chestnut nape

◄ Breeding ♂ is unmistakable

Note face and back pattern from rear

◄ Juv's yellow bill, more strongly patterned plumage and double wing-bars distinguish it from the Reed Bunting

Longer wing tip (cp Reed Bunting)

Black "triangle" (juv also)

♀ and juv are very like Reed Bunting but curious face pattern shows well in the field

White outer tail

Bill, plumage, facial pattern and long wings and tail are keys to distinguishing Lapland Bunting. "Creeping" feeder, often occurring on or near coast with Shore Larks or Snow Buntings. Typical swift, often high bunting flight. *Very clear "ticky-tik-tiu" call, also rattling ticking call.* Annual winter visitor, mainly to E coast.

Open Country and Woodland Birds

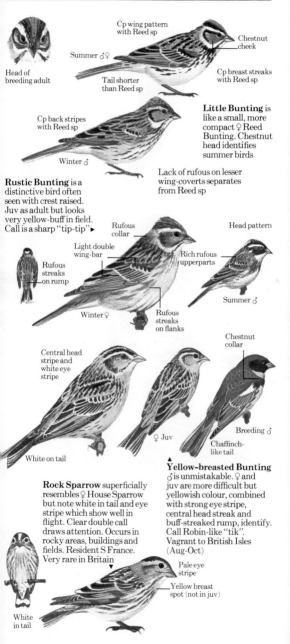

Cp wing pattern with Reed sp

Chestnut cheek

Summer ♂♀

Head of breeding adult

Cp breast streaks with Reed sp

Tail shorter than Reed sp

Cp back stripes with Reed sp

Winter ♂

Little Bunting is like a small, more compact ♀ Reed Bunting. Chestnut head identifies summer birds

Rustic Bunting is a distinctive bird often seen with crest raised. Juv as adult but looks very yellow-buff in field. Call is a sharp "tip-tip" ▶

Lack of rufous on lesser wing-coverts separates from Reed sp

Rufous streaks on rump

Rufous collar

Light double wing-bar

Rich rufous upperparts

Head pattern

Winter ♀

Rufous streaks on flanks

Summer ♂

Central head stripe and white eye stripe

Chestnut collar

White on tail

♀ Juv

Chaffinch-like tail

Breeding ♂

Yellow-breasted Bunting ♂ is unmistakable. ♀ and juv are more difficult but yellowish colour, combined with strong eye streak, central head streak and buff-streaked rump, identify. Call Robin-like "tik". Vagrant to British Isles (Aug-Oct)

Rock Sparrow superficially resembles ♀ House Sparrow but note white in tail and eye stripe which show well in flight. Clear double call draws attention. Occurs in rocky areas, buildings and fields. Resident S France. Very rare in Britain ▼

Pale eye stripe

Yellow breast spot (not in juv)

White in tail

47

Snow Bunting

Juv plumage has least amount of white in wings. Note face pattern ▼

Adult ♂ winter

Imm ♂ winter

White markings on long wings are unlike any other bird but Snow Finch (confined to Alps)

Wing pattern flickers in flight

White in tail

Buff plumage wears to produce ◄ breeding dress

Adult ♂ summer

Breeding ♀ has ► streaked back

All birds have dark eye set in a pale face with dark crown and darkish face patch. Note thin white streak ◄ on juv (wider on ♂)

Imm ♂

Party feeding on beach

Large bunting with very long wings which reach almost to tip of tail. Tame and unobtrusive, taking flight only at last moment. Before adulthood, plumage undergoes a series of complex changes. Flocking birds on wing make eye-catching patterns of black and white, accompanied by loud, tinkling calls. Flight is fast with occasional erratic low swoops over shingle. Call is a rippling "tirrirrir-rip", with "seeoo" or "swapeck" calls from flock. Apart from a few localities in Scottish mountains and Norway, breeds only in Arctic. Frequent winter visitor (Oct-Mar) to E coast of Britain and forms flocks on inland hills in N, with individuals occurring elsewhere.

Horned Lark

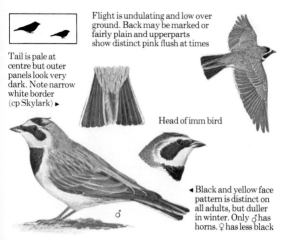

Flight is undulating and low over ground. Back may be marked or fairly plain and upperparts show distinct pink flush at times

Tail is pale at centre but outer panels look very dark. Note narrow white border (cp Skylark) ▶

Head of imm bird

♂

◀ Black and yellow face pattern is distinct on all adults, but duller in winter. Only ♂ has horns. ♀ has less black

Easily identified by face pattern. Feeds on shingle and marshy areas of coastal wasteland, blending well with ground and usually only seen when flushed. Soft, rippling flight call. Has nested in Scotland but occurs mainly on E coast (Oct-Apr), usually in small parties or flocks, often with Snow and Lapland Buntings.

Snow Finch

Summer

Vivid contrast of black and white shows clearly on underwing and from above

Large white area in tail (cp Snow Bunting)

Summer ♂ and ♀ have chocolate back and black bill

Winter

Streaked back

Very long wings

Yellow bill (winter)

Grey head and black chin of summer birds separate from Snow Bunting. Winter birds are less clearly marked on back and throat

Common on the scree and rocky gullies of S Europe's high mountains. Can only be confused with Snow Bunting but they are very unlikely to occur together. Upright stance except when feeding, which is confined to ground. Attracted to man by food and descends to lower altitudes in winter. Very rare outside its breeding area and has not occurred in British Isles.

49

Woodlark

Typical flight attitudes show broad, stubby wings

White eye stripe, and streaked breast contrasting with paler belly show well on birds of all ages

Bold crest is ▲ often raised and dropped

Black and white

Short tail and marked back streaking show well on adults. Plumage wear results in paler look

Dumpy build and jerkier movements in flight distinguish Woodlark from longer-winged and tailed Skylark. Circling song flight at one level before descent. (Skylark continues rising vertically until out of sight.) *Flute-like song and "titlooeet" flight call.* Confined to heath and scrub in S England; decreasing.

Short-toed Larks

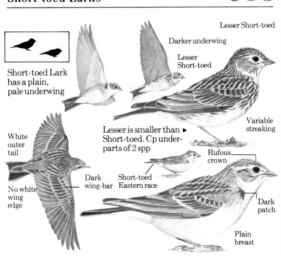

Lesser Short-toed

Darker underwing

Lesser Short-toed

Short-toed Lark has a plain, pale underwing

White outer tail

No white wing edge

Lesser is smaller than ▶ Short-toed. Cp under-parts of 2 spp

Dark wing-bar

Short-toed Eastern race

Variable streaking

Rufous crown

Dark patch

Plain breast

Small, fast, low-flying larks, instantly *distinguished from Skylark by lack of white on trailing edge.* Birds of open country, often overlooked as they run along ground (often at great speed). Form ground-skimming flocks which tend to land together abruptly. "Chirrup" and "wee-oo" calls. Both species are vagrants, occasionally occurring in flocks.

Skylark

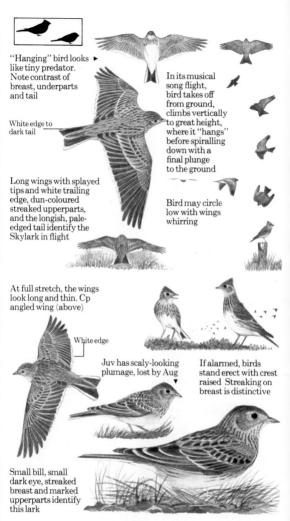

"Hanging" bird looks like tiny predator. Note contrast of breast, underparts and tail

White edge to dark tail

In its musical song flight, bird takes off from ground, climbs vertically to great height, where it "hangs" before spiralling down with a final plunge to the ground

Long wings with splayed tips and white trailing edge, dun-coloured streaked upperparts, and the longish, pale-edged tail identify the Skylark in flight

Bird may circle low with wings whirring

At full stretch, the wings look long and thin. Cp angled wing (above)

White edge

Juv has scaly-looking plumage, lost by Aug

If alarmed, birds stand erect with crest raised Streaking on breast is distinctive

Small bill, small dark eye, streaked breast and marked upperparts identify this lark

An easily identifiable bird and one of the commonest in the British Isles, but with more flight actions and profiles than any other small bird. *Differs from other larks in its longer wings and tail and well-proportioned shape.* Prolonged flight is a series of long, shallow, erratic undulations with a pattern of several wingbeats followed by wing closure. Call is a rolling chirrup, constantly uttered by flying birds. Melodious, bubbling song is uttered from perch as well as on wing. Can occur singly, but, Oct-Mar especially, is seen in either small parties or enormous flocks, usually over arable land, but sometimes over any open country. There is an enormous influx of larks from Continent in Oct-Nov.

Crested Lark

Heavy build ▶
but buoyant
flight

Orange
armpit

Orange
outer
tail

Orange outer
tail

Prominent
crest

Juv has smaller
crest and less
orange in tail

Heavy bill

Broad wings ▶
show in flight

Large crest,
which is often
raised, and
dark patch at
top of breast
are distinctive

Long legs

Shape is rounder
in the cold

Robust, rather coarse-featured lark with a crest, bill and outer tail that distinguish it from any other lark. Flight is undulating but surprisingly buoyant for its build. Call a distinct, liquid "swee-er-wee". Bird of open country, roadsides and urban areas, commonly seen on Continent, but very rare in Britain.

Corn Bunting

Note large
size and lack
of white in tail

Coarse
bill

Legs
dangled

Streaks on
breast and
throat show well

Head is back and ▶
seed-cracking bill
open as it sings

Heavy build, odd bill shape and
fine streaking are distinctive

Largest and coarsest-looking of the buntings, to be seen perching conspicuously on wires and fence posts or feeding quietly on ground. Male dangles legs as it flutters off perch in breeding season. *Song like jangling keys,* and sharp "quit" call note. Occurs in open, usually arable, country throughout British Isles.

Tawny Pipit

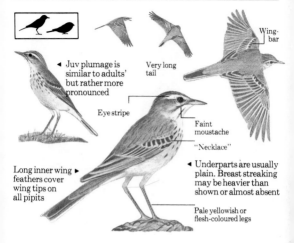

◄ Juv plumage is similar to adults' but rather more pronounced

Very long tail

Wing-bar

Eye stripe

Faint moustache

"Necklace"

Long inner wing ► feathers cover wing tips on all pipits

◄ Underparts are usually plain. Breast streaking may be heavier than shown or almost absent

Pale yellowish or flesh-coloured legs

Slim, elegant bird very like a sort of buff wagtail. Pale eye stripe, dark line through eye and lack of heavy breast streaking distinguish Tawny from all other pipits. Flight very undulating and direct. *Drawn-out wagtail-like "sweep" call and rolling chirrup* draw instant attention. Vagrant, mainly S and SE England (Apr-Nov latest).

Red-throated Pipit

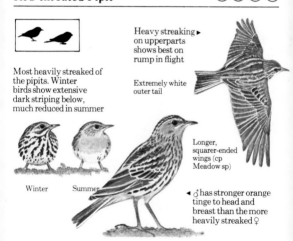

Heavy streaking ► on upperparts shows best on rump in flight

Most heavily streaked of the pipits. Winter birds show extensive dark striping below, much reduced in summer

Extremely white outer tail

Winter   Summer

Longer, squarer-ended wings (cp Meadow sp)

◄ ♂ has stronger orange tinge to head and breast than the more heavily streaked ♀

Size, shape, plumage and behaviour is very similar to Meadow Pipit but heavier streaking, orange throat (in breeding season), *absence of greenish tinge,* and its very explosive "chup" call distinguish the Red-throated Pipit. Also has "tseez" call not unlike Tree Pipit. Rare vagrant (2-3 per year) in British Isles.

Meadow Pipit

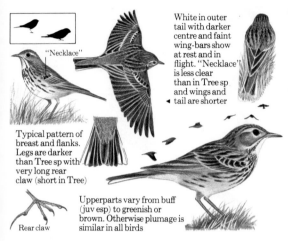

"Necklace"

White in outer tail with darker centre and faint wing-bars show at rest and in flight. "Necklace" is less clear than in Tree sp and wings and ◀ tail are shorter

Typical pattern of breast and flanks. Legs are darker than Tree sp with very long rear claw (short in Tree)

Rear claw

Upperparts vary from buff (juv esp) to greenish or brown. Otherwise plumage is similar in all birds

Commonest of the pipits, to be seen rising erratically with characteristic "tsiip-tsiip-tsiip" call from rough ground throughout the British Isles. Small flocks seem to "see-saw" in air as if struggling for height. Ground feeders which, if flushed, return to ground, but will perch in trees. Found on moorland, waste and (especially in winter) fields and coast.

Tree Pipit

Ascends and then "parachutes" back to same or near perch in song flight

White outer tail

◀ Back pattern is like Meadow sp but never as greenish or yellowish

Wings and tail longer than Meadow

Pronounced "necklace" (cp Meadow)

Erratic, undulating flight like Meadow sp but "teez" call is unlike Meadow's call

Like Meadow sp but with larger "necklace" on wing, more buff breast and larger, more spaced spots. Legs are brighter flesh colour (dark in Meadow)

Very like Meadow Pipit but *stockier build, pronounced "necklace" on wing and more erect stance* help to distinguish. Takes refuge in tree if flushed, but feeds only on ground. Wags tail which distinguishes it from larks. *"Teez" flight call is diagnostic.* Found in heathland with scattered trees throughout Britain (Apr-Oct).

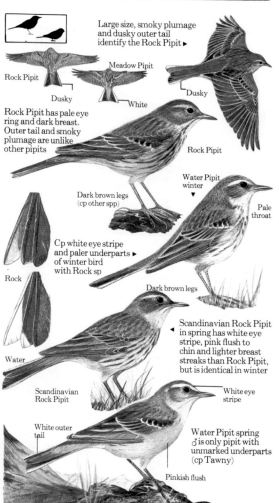

Large size, smoky plumage and dusky outer tail identify the Rock Pipit ▶

Rock Pipit

Meadow Pipit

Dusky

White

Dusky

Rock Pipit has pale eye ring and dark breast. Outer tail and smoky plumage are unlike other pipits

Rock Pipit

Water Pipit winter ▼

Dark brown legs (cp other spp)

Pale throat

Cp white eye stripe and paler underparts ▶ of winter bird with Rock sp

Rock

Dark brown legs

Water

◀ Scandinavian Rock Pipit in spring has white eye stripe, pink flush to chin and lighter breast streaks than Rock Pipit, but is identical in winter

Scandinavian Rock Pipit

White eye stripe

White outer tail

Water Pipit spring ♂ is only pipit with unmarked underparts (cp Tawny)

Pinkish flush

The Rock Pipit is much larger than the ubiquitous Meadow Pipit, but its extremely dark plumage makes it difficult to see against rocky coastal habitat. Similar to Tree Pipit in its deliberate gait, undulating flight and tail-wagging with a distinct "tsup" call more akin to Tree Pipit call than shrill sound of Meadow species. Young birds are more streaked than adults. Rock Pipit is resident, seen mainly in rocky coastal areas in breeding season, and coastal or wet areas inland in winter. Water Pipits, which breed in mountains of Eurasia, are winter visitors (Sept-Apr), occur in ones and twos and are usually coastal, but may be seen in wet areas inland such as cress beds and sewage farms.

Grey Wagtail

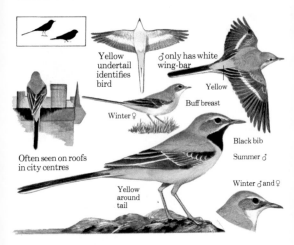

Yellow undertail identifies bird

♂ only has white wing-bar

Yellow

Buff breast

Winter ♀

Often seen on roofs in city centres

Black bib

Summer ♂

Winter ♂ and ♀

Yellow around tail

Grey upperparts contrasting with yellow underparts are distinctive. *Yellow encircles tail at all times of year.* Largest tailed and slimmest winged of wagtails with dipping, exaggerated flight and tail constantly wagging. Sharp "tizpeep" call. Occurs throughout British Isles but less common in parts of England.

Yellow Wagtail

All-yellow

Adult ♀

White outer tail visible in flight

Blue-headed ♂

♀s of all forms are alike

♂ (Britain)

Scandinavian form ♂

White outer tail

Brilliance and extent of yellow vary widely in ♂'s

Juvs of all forms are alike. Note throat marks

Bright yellow-headed form is commonest in Britain, but blue-headed form also occurs in SE (only males differ). Active birds tail-wagging and darting after insects on ground. Dipping, skipping flight. *Distinctive "tsweep" call.* Found in watery meadows and a few drier habitats (Apr-Sept) in Britain S of Clyde. Very rare in Ireland.

♂ Pied looks almost black on back in summer, greyer in winter. Wing-bars are prominent in ♂ and ♀ ▶

Black nape

Pied Wagtail

Grey back and rump in ♂ and ♀

White Wagtail

Summer ♂

♂

Sparkling grey of White summer ♂ is enhanced by touches of black. White Wagtails are regular but scarce visitors to Britain

Juv White and ▶ Pied look alike. Note breast pattern

Pied summer ♂ is black and white with smoky grey flank feathers

Sometimes grey

Clear grey rump

1st yr White Wagtail

White Wagtail in first ▶ year. Crown on some birds is clear grey. Flanks on ♂, ♀ and juv are pale grey

Black rump

♀

◀ Pied Wagtail ♀ has dark grey back, with olive-grey tinge in some birds, but black rump distinguishes it from White Wagtail

Pied Wagtail plumage is very variable and can look similar to that of White, but White Wagtails are continental birds passing through Britain only in Mar-May and Aug-Oct and are regular only in the west. *Thus all black and white Wagtails seen in winter will be Pied, and almost all those seen in the summer.* The deliberate gait, and bobbing and wagging tail are familiar sights on open land in town and country (including lawns, roads and roofs) throughout the British Isles. Typical undulating wagtail flight. Call a distinct shrill "chizzick". Nests in holes, walls and sheds. White Wagtail has bred in Britain (very rare), and Pied and White Wagtail crosses occur.

Alpine Accentor

Dark double wing-bar

Stronger bill (cp Dunnock)

Juv

♂ and ♀ Accentors ► have dark double bands on their wings. In fresh plumage these are edged with pale or white feathers which wear off. Note speckled throat

Buff tip to ta

Adults have well-defined area of throat speckles which is lacking in juv

Brightly streaked flanks

Dunnock

A quiet, unobtrusive bird, much *larger and more stoutly built than the closely related Dunnock* (see plumage differences). Inhabits rocky mountain slopes and alpine meadows, descending to lower altitudes in winter. Faintly lark-like flight is low and undulating. Call is a "turrip-rip" not unlike Dunnock. Very rare vagrant to Britain, mainly to S England and usually in winter.

Wallcreeper

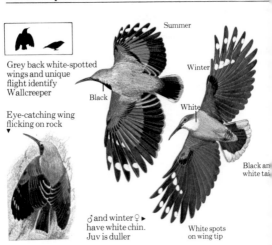

Grey back white-spotted wings and unique flight identify Wallcreeper

Summer

Winter

Black

White

Eye-catching wing flicking on rock ▼

Black and white tai

♂ and winter ♀ ► have white chin. Juv is duller

White spots on wing tip

Very long, broad, rounded wings and rich plumage colours make the Wallcreeper unmistakable. Digs insects out of crevices with its long decurved bill. Curious wing flicking while perched is a feature to be seen on the mountain rockfaces, quarries and buildings of its continental habitat. Very rare vagrant to Britain (winters in quarries and sea cliffs).

Red tail

Autumn ♂ is duller, with less white and more mottled back

Orange armpit

♀

Striped throat

Crescent marks

♀

Spring ♂ has vivid orange underparts and blue-grey head and mantle

Posture more like Wheatear than Thrush

Blue Rock Thrush

♂ (Aug-Sept)

Long square tail

Juv Blue Rock Thrush has buff, spotted throat ▼

Blue Rock Thrushes ng from buildings

♀ Blue Rock Thrush is a dullish brown above with ◀ blue-grey tinge

♂

Juv Blue Rock Thrush

Blue Rock Thrush is blue-grey overall with slightly darker wings and tail. ♀ has blue-grey tinge above with pale, mottled underparts

The Rock Thrush is a wary bird, quick to take swift flight down a hillside, and displaying the nervous, busy actions of a chat. The Blue Rock Thrush more secure and relaxed in its behaviour, with a warm, melodious song and disposition similar to the Blackbird's. The Rock Thrush is found in mountainous areas of W Europe whereas the Blue Rock species occurs from sea level in any rocky, barren areas and frequents towns in S Europe, where it replaces the Blackbird. The northern limit of both species is S central France, but the Rock Thrush is migratory and occurs very rarely in Britain. Only one record of the sedentary Blue Rock Thrush occurring in Britain exists.

Song Thrush

Absence of marks (cp Mistle)

Orange underwing

Song Thrush

Redwing

No obvious marks on back. Very ◄ like Redwing

Singing in tree. (Mistle Thrush prefers treetop perch for song)

Creamy yellow, heavily spotted underparts

Typical feeding action on lawn

Pale legs

The standard garden thrush, with arrow-shaped breast spots, crescen behind eye and dark streak on either side of throat distinguishing it from Mistle Thrush. Feeding behaviour is distinctive —hops, interspersed with short runs, are broken by upright, watchful pauses. "Tick" or "tsip" fligh call and song of repeated phrases. Common throughout British Isles.

Mistle Thrush

Note long-winged, pot-bellied profile

Bolder pattern (cp Song sp)

Paler rump

Small head

Heavy build and shape differ from Song sp. Long wings are often drooped

Long white-tipped tail

Pale edges to wings contrast with uniform ◄ back of Song sp

White underwing

Splayed wing tips

Largest and boldest of thrushes. Pot belly and long wings and tail in fligh together with very upright, barrel-chested stance on ground a distinctive. Deeply undulating flight with periodic closure of wings. Lou chattering *"football-rattle" call* and ringing song with no repeated phrase Wide but patchy distribution throughout British Isles.

Similar to Song Thrush above, red underwing may be seen (cp orange in Thrush)

Flight is often swift and erratic. Plumage identifies if seen from below

right red underwing   White   Forked tail

common view; eye stripe and marks on wings are eye-catching

Song Thrush

Prominent eye stripe

◄ Red flanks, eye stripe and heavily streaked underparts show at close range

Redwing   Yellow

smallest and darkest of the thrushes, to be seen feeding gregariously in open lds. Generally retiring and only comes to gardens in severe weather. nall-looking in flight with characteristic wing-flicking action. Hops hen feeding on ground. Takes berries (eg Hawthorn). *Penetrating "steep"* ll. Visitor in huge numbers (Oct-Apr). Breeds in Scotland.

Contrasting tail and rump

Loose flocks are typical of the sp. Waving, erratic flight resembles Mistle Thrush

white underwing gnostic

Dark patch

Grey rump and dark tail show on take-off

Typical view in field showing grey rump ◄ and black tail

Black tail

Note contrast of creamy, spotted breast, grey head and rufous back on ♂ and ♀

White underwing

rger than Song Thrush with long wings and tail. *Resembles Mistle rush in build and flight.* Feeds on berries or on open ground in fields and, severe weather, gardens. Extremely wary bird with harsh chattering a-cha-chack" call. Common winter visitor (Oct-Apr) throughout tish Isles and now breeding sporadically from Shetland to Pennines.

Blackbird

Splayed wings

Flicking, gliding flight, and profile, identify Blackbird

Sings its lovely song from roof, tree or wall ♂

Long tail

Jerky flight is completed by tail-raising on landing

Round tail

♀

Cp shape and long profile with Starling

♀ is a dark brown version of the ♂

Pale throat

Black tail

Rufous brown

♀

Jet-black ♂ has yellow eye ring and bill. Bill has brown tip in winter

♂

The male is the only thrush and common garden bird that is jet black. Juven is like a ginger-bodied female, but shape identifies it. Noisy, excitable bir given to much tail-flicking, with a rattling alarm call, low "tchoo tchook" call and "chink" call at dusk. Many whitish mutations occu Very common throughout British Isles and a winter visitor.

Ring Ouzel

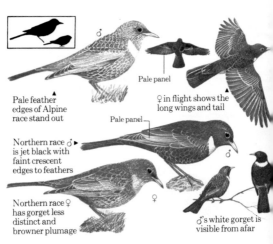

♂

Pale panel

Pale feather edges of Alpine race stand out

♀ in flight shows the long wings and tail

Pale panel

Northern race ♂ is jet black with faint crescent edges to feathers

♂

Northern race ♀ has gorget less distinct and browner plumage

♀

♂'s white gorget is visible from afar

Moorland counterpart of Blackbird and similar in behaviour a appearance, but for longer wings and tail and plumage differenc Confusable with Blackbird mutations. Shy, normally shunning hat tation. Flight wild and dashing. Harsh "chack-chack" call and clear, f carrying song. Only Northern race occurs (Mar-Oct). Some birds winte

◄ Flight is swift and direct with a series of wing-beats followed by a glide

Starlings have a sharp profile in flight with noticeably fan-shaped tail

Only bird that sings with open mouth and wings flapping slowly ►

Contrast between pale underwing and black underparts shows well in flight and distinguishes Starling from ◄ Blackbird

Pale round tail

Juv is grey-brown ► with pale throat. Acquires semi-juv semi-adult plumage later. Actions just like adults

Typical view of a group sitting in a tree

Heavily marked all over

Reddish legs

Noisy, squabbling, quarrelsome birds, extremely fat-looking when relaxed. The only bird that pecks at ground with open bill when lawn feeding

Cp Starling's actions with other garden birds. Its bustling, upright waddle is unlike the hesitant, intermittent actions of Thrush and Blackbird

Song Thrush   Starling   Blackbird

Cp totally different shapes of these 3 common garden visitors.

Aggressive, garrulous, dumpy birds, to be seen carrolling and chattering away on rooftops or swooping down to vie for hand-outs. Heavily marked plumage is glossy and iridescent with buff-tipped back feathers, spotted underparts and heavily spotted, almost greyish head. Plumage wears to become almost black in spring. Long bill is bright yellow in spring and fuller in winter. Plumage, shape, behaviour and very wide vocabulary of songs and calls (generally a harsh churring call and pleasant gurgling song) make the Starling one of the most distinctive garden visitors. Very common throughout the British Isles in all urban and agricultural habitats. Vast influx from Continent in winter.

Waxwing

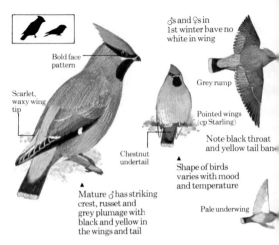

♂s and ♀s in 1st winter have no white in wing

Bold face pattern

Scarlet, waxy wing tip

Grey rump

Pointed wings (cp Starling)

Note black throat and yellow tail band

Chestnut undertail

Shape of birds varies with mood and temperature

▲ Mature ♂ has striking crest, russet and grey plumage with black and yellow in the wings and tail

Pale underwing

Prominent crest, faint trilling call and often conspicuous behaviour draw attention to the Waxwing. Starling-sized with buoyant Starling-like flight, but dumpier in the body with longer wings and tail. Feeds on berries such as Hawthorn and Cotoneaster in heathland, gardens and roadsides. A few occur most years, usually in parties, Oct-Apr.

Golden Oriole

Leisurely, deeply undulating flight and vivid plumage of ♂ are unique

Old ♀

Black area round eye

♂

♂

♂

♀ and juv

♀

Juv

Heavily streaked

Extremely shy birds, often very difficult to see in tree foliage, although brilliantly coloured male and yellows, greens and blacks of female and young are unmistakable. Old female is like male but lacks black area round eye. Male has a "wheela-wheeo" call and female's is a harsh "quik-quik-quik". Few passage birds occur Apr-Aug; now breeds in England.

Lesser/Great Grey Shrike

Lesser Grey Shrike has narrow, pointed wings with large, well-defined white wing panels

Black

Extent of black

Panels variable

Grey

◄ Great Grey Shrike has broad, rounded wings with variable white panels and very splayed wing tips of uneven length

Extent of black

Lesser Grey

Great Grey

Lesser Grey

Juv Lesser Grey ◄ has no black on forehead. Wing shape separates from Great Grey

Lesser Grey in typical ▶ upright perching attitude. Black forehead and pinkish wash on breast are very obvious

Shrikes holding prey and feeding. Prey is held in the foot and impaled on thorns, to make a "larder"

◄ Grey forehead and white lining between back and wing separate Great Grey from Lesser Grey. At rest or in flight, its greater tail length is very noticeable

White (absent on Lesser Grey)

Great Grey

Long wing tip

Lesser Grey's very long primary feathers and shortish tail give it a different appearance from the stubby winged Great Grey. Areas of white and black also differ ▶

Lesser Grey

The Great Grey is the largest of the European shrikes, and feeds on small mammals, birds and large beetles. The Lesser Grey is mainly insectivorous in its diet. Shape and differing combinations of black, white and grey in plumage distinguish the two species. Both tend to perch very conspicuously on wires or bushes, turning head from side to side on lookout for prey. Flight over a distance looks curiously feeble and undulating, although the Great Grey catches birds on wing. Both have typical "chiuk-chiuk" Shrike call. Great Grey is a solitary winter visitor to Britain (especially in E) Oct-Apr. Lesser Grey is rare in Britain, May-Oct (about 3 or 4 per year).

Woodchat

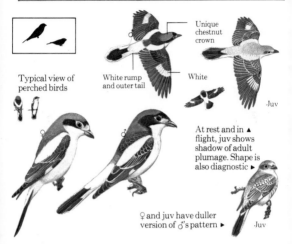

Typical view of perched birds

Unique chestnut crown

White rump and outer tail

White

Juv

At rest and in ▲ flight, juv shows shadow of adult plumage. Shape is also diagnostic ▶

♀ and juv have duller version of ♂'s pattern ▶

Juv

Rounder-headed, broader-winged and shorter-tailed shrike than Red-backed species. Adult plumage is unmistakable and juvenile is always identifiable by shape, especially of head, bill and tail. Often perches on wires but will also sit unobtrusively in a bush. Behaviour and harsh call typically shrike-like. Scarce but regular visitor to British Isles (Apr-Oct).

Red-backed Shrike

Juv

♀

♂

Direct flight with frequent glides

♂

Note crescent marks on orange-brown juv and typical shrike bill
▼

Grey, black and white of ♂'s head, tail and rump contrast with its red back
▼

Black mask

Often pink flush

Crescent marks

Juv

♂

♀

♀

♀ has rich red upperparts like ♂ but no black in tail

Smallest and slimmest of the shrikes with rather long, pointed wings and long tail. Behaviour is typical of shrikes, and includes impaling of prey. Prolonged flights are undulating. Call is a swearing "cheeuk-cheeuk". Summer visitor (May-Sept), once quite common, but decreasing. Now only 50 pairs in SE England and a few passage visitors to coast (Aug-Sept).

House Martin

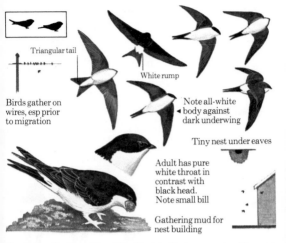

Triangular tail

Birds gather on wires, esp prior to migration

White rump

Note all-white body against dark underwing ◄

Tiny nest under eaves

Adult has pure white throat in contrast with black head. Note small bill

Gathering mud for nest building

Smaller than Swallow, with steel-blue (black-looking) upperparts, white rump and white underparts from chin to tail. Avid feeder, usually low over water on arrival, but in general higher than Swallow. Flicking wing action in its wheeling flight. "Tchirrup" call. Summer visitor (Apr-mid-Nov) throughout British Isles. Some late broods abandoned by adults.

Sand Martin

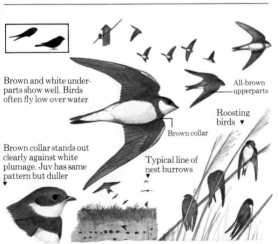

Brown and white underparts show well. Birds often fly low over water

All-brown upperparts

Roosting birds ▼

Brown collar stands out clearly against white plumage. Juv has same pattern but duller ▼

Brown collar

Typical line of nest burrows ▼

Smallest of the "swallows", with unmistakable plumage pattern unique in a bird of its size. Often the first arrival (summer visitor, Mar-Oct), to be seen feeding over lakes and reservoirs. More direct and flicking flight than House Martin. Hard, harsh, rippling call. Breeds in any vertical, exposed bank or excavation. Roosts in reed beds in spring and autumn.

Swallow

Deeply forked tail

Pinkish buff underparts (pure white in Sand Martin), very long, well-forked tail and steel-blue upperparts distinguish Swallow from all other birds. It may sometimes be difficult to see the whole length of the tail

Red forehead

High-flying birds have an easy, slow, floating action as they feed and the flight is slower than when feeding at low level. Flight action is more level than the swoops and turns of martins. Migrating birds may be seen following the coastline in great numbers

Juv   ♀   ♂

Swallows congregate in excitable groups, esp before migration. Juv is paler than the adult with a markedly shorter tail. ♀'s tail streamers are shorter than those of the adult ♂, which are variable in length

Red face standing out against blue upperparts and collar is a key identification feature. Juv's plumage is less vivid

Low-level insect-catching flight is a common sight in early summer in parks and fields

The Swallow, like the Swift and House Martin, is closely associated with man, nesting in buildings such as barns and outhouses, reaching the nest unerringly and at high speed through an often very narrow opening. Pairs tend to return to the same nest. *Distinguished from swifts and martins by flight, plumage and tail length.* Spends a great deal of time in the air, but often seen perched on wires or fences. Lands to gather mud for nest building. Call is emphatic "tswit-tswit" and song a repeated twittering "feeta-feet". Widespread summer visitor (Apr-Oct). Very early arrivals Mar and stragglers until Nov, especially in the west. Large numbers of migrating birds may be seen following coastline.

Swift

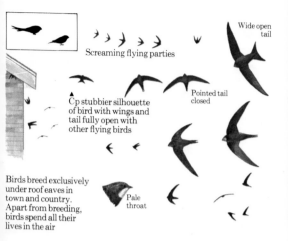

Screaming flying parties

Wide open tail

Pointed tail closed

▲ Cp stubbier silhouette of bird with wings and tail fully open with other flying birds

Pale throat

Birds breed exclusively under roof eaves in town and country. Apart from breeding, birds spend all their lives in the air

The most aerial of all species, built for speed, and unmistakable in its torpedo body, scimitar-shaped wings and dark brown (but black-looking) plumage. Pale underwings will flash in sun. Rapid, windmilling wing-beats in careering flight. Distinctive high, thin scream, especially in fading light. Seen everywhere late Apr-end Aug (stragglers until Oct).

Alpine Swift

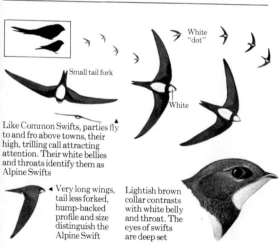

White "dot"

Small tail fork

White

Like Common Swifts, parties fly to and fro above towns, their high, trilling call attracting attention. Their white bellies and throats identify them as Alpine Swifts

◄ Very long wings, tail less forked, hump-backed profile and size distinguish the Alpine Swift

Lightish brown collar contrasts with white belly and throat. The eyes of swifts are deep set

Largest of the European swifts (twice the Common Swift's weight) with plumage much less dark. Seen morning and evening especially in built-up areas, but also frequents mountains and cliffs down to sea level. Flight as Common Swift but faster and more vigorous. *High trilling call.* Nest in holes and roof eaves. Vagrant in British Isles (Apr-Oct).

Dipper

Flies rapidly up and down following line of stream

White eyelid

Black belly

European race

Bobbing and tail-cocking and white breast against blackish plumage identify adults ▼

Swimming bird

British race

Rufous belly

◄ Juv is grey above with more white below

Never seen away from the swift streams, lake edges or pools of its moorland or upland habitat. A few winter in lowland areas. Plump shape, and behaviour, which includes swimming, and *feeding on stream bed*, are unmistakable. Flight generally fast and whirring. Call loud "zit-zit-zit". Found in suitable habitat W of line from Humber to Solent.

Kingfisher

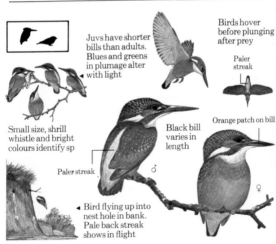

Juvs have shorter bills than adults. Blues and greens in plumage alter ◄ with light

Birds hover before plunging after prey

Paler streak

Small size, shrill whistle and bright colours identify sp

Black bill varies in length

Orange patch on bill

Paler streak

♂

♀

◄ Bird flying up into nest hole in bank. Pale back streak shows in flight

Usually seen in flight as a blue streak following line of river or stream. Often perches on branch just above water. Will dive straight from perch or hover to sight prey. High-flying spring display. Often found by very small streams in winter. Generally distributed throughout British Isles, although absent from much of N Scotland.

Turtle Dove

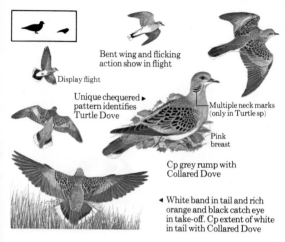

Bent wing and flicking action show in flight

Display flight

Unique chequered ▶ pattern identifies Turtle Dove

Multiple neck marks (only in Turtle sp)

Pink breast

Cp grey rump with Collared Dove

◀ White band in tail and rich orange and black catch eye in take-off. Cp extent of white in tail with Collared Dove

Smallest of the European doves. Feeds on ground and nests low down in bushes and hedges. Most often seen in flight, which is very swift and direct with curious intermittent tilting. Soaring display flight. Soft, purring "rooorrr-roorrr". Found in farmland and open country, including large gardens, S of Tyne-Morecambe Bay and S Ireland. Visitor (Apr-Oct).

Collared Dove

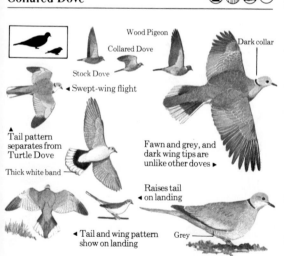

Wood Pigeon

Collared Dove

Dark collar

Stock Dove

◀ Swept-wing flight

▲ Tail pattern separates from Turtle Dove

Thick white band

Fawn and grey, and dark wing tips are unlike other doves ▶

Raises tail ◀ on landing

◀ Tail and wing pattern show on landing

Grey

A heavy dove, very pale with long tail and broad wings, which are held back in its deliberate, flicking flight. In display, rises almost vertically and sails round on spread wings. Ground feeding and other habits very like pigeons. *Irritating "coo, coo, cuck" call, and buzzing nasal display note*. First nested in 1955, now distributed throughout British Isles.

Rock Dove

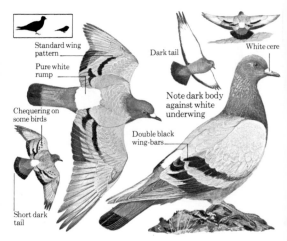

Standard wing pattern

Pure white rump

Chequering on some birds

Short dark tail

Dark tail

White cere

Note dark body against white underwing

Double black wing-bars

Ancestor of all domestic pigeons. Pure flocks likely to be all blue with a few natural chequers. Any other plumage variation indicates interbreeding. Male has glossier green neck than female. *Blue-grey skin round eye and white cere* on bill. Very broad shouldered in profile. Seems to occur mainly on N and W coasts of Scotland and Atlantic coasts of Ireland.

Feral Pigeon

Feral Pigeons have typical sailing display flight often preceded by slow, deliberate flaps of wings

Stouter bill (cp Rock Dove)

Feral Pigeon in plumage phase which most resembles Rock Dove. Birds are almost identical ▼

Chequering

Town or Feral ► Pigeons occur in every sort of plumage from white through chequer patterns to black. They have stouter bills than the Rock Dove

Domesticated descendant of the Rock Dove occurring in a wide variety of forms throughout the British Isles. Flocks may sometimes be seen in fields feeding with racing pigeons. Often seen with Jackdaws on large, ornate buildings which provide breeding ledges. Extended breeding season, nesting through winter, as a result of abundant food supply in towns.

Wood Pigeon

Vigorous wingbeats, pot-belly and white patch show well

Very large white patch on wing and dark outer half show in flight. White collar also stands out well

White neck patch

Birds take off with great clatter of wings. Note white patches

Grey inner wing

Black-banded tail and pinkish breast show well from below

Wings are held back emphasizing body shape. Note white ◀ collar

Bow-winged display flight

Smallness of head accentuates ▶ stocky look of body. Note tail extending beyond wings (cp Stock Dove)

White

Pink

White wing patch

Largest and *commonest pigeon in the British Isles and the only one with white collar and large white wing panels.* Large body, deep chest and small, erect head also distinguish from other pigeons. Often seen flocking in huge numbers in autumn and winter. Feeds in fields and woodlands. Can be extremely tame or very wary, depending on treatment by man. Commonly seen in cities and towns with feral pigeons. Flight is swift and direct, with hesitant approach when landing in tree. Widespread tail conspicuous on landing. In courtship flight rises steeply, claps wings and sails around in display. Call is the familiar "coor-cooo, coor-cooo'. Resident throughout British Isles.

Stock Dove

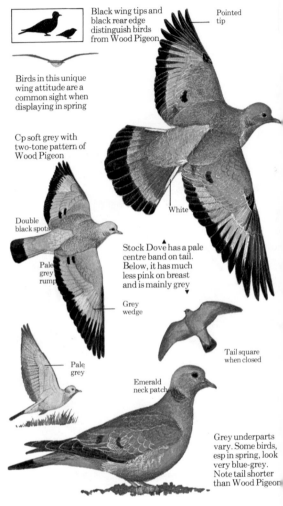

Black wing tips and black rear edge distinguish birds from Wood Pigeon

Pointed tip

Birds in this unique wing attitude are a common sight when displaying in spring

Cp soft grey with two-tone pattern of Wood Pigeon

Double black spots

Pale grey rump

White

Stock Dove has a pale centre band on tail. Below, it has much less pink on breast and is mainly grey

Grey wedge

Tail square when closed

Pale grey

Emerald neck patch

Grey underparts vary. Some birds, esp in spring, look very blue-grey. Note tail shorter than Wood Pigeon

Smaller and more compact than Wood Pigeon, with squarer head and no significant areas of white visible when observed in the field. Wings are narrower, almost triangular, with straighter rear surface than on Wood Pigeon. Usually seen in pairs but flocks do occur. Flight is swift and direct with wings held straighter than Wood Pigeon and with intermittent slight flicking action. Soars on angled wings in display flight. Call is a monotonous regular "rroo-roo-ro". Nests in holes in trees, or occasionally in buildings (especially in Ireland). Found in woods and farmland throughout British Isles (except NW Scotland) and formerly common in urban parks. Reduced in numbers by pesticides but now increasing.

Nuthatch

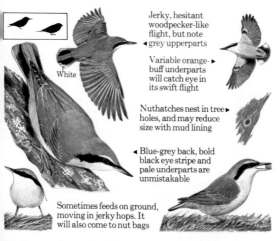

Jerky, hesitant woodpecker-like flight, but note ◄ grey upperparts

Variable orange-buff underparts ► will catch eye in its swift flight

White

Nuthatches nest in tree ► holes, and may reduce size with mud lining

◄ Blue-grey back, bold black eye stripe and pale underparts are unmistakable

Sometimes feeds on ground, moving in jerky hops. It will also come to nut bags

Ebullient, restless, noisy bird. Loud whistling call "hweet-hweet", constant movement up, down and around branches and trunks, and demonic facial expression are unmistakable. Will suddenly take swift flight. Often only a silhouette of flying birds is visible. Found in deciduous woodland, including wooded gardens, in Britain S of Tees-Solway.

Wryneck

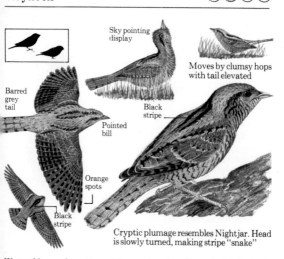

Sky pointing display

Moves by clumsy hops with tail elevated

Barred grey tail

Black stripe

Pointed bill

Orange spots

Black stripe

Cryptic plumage resembles Nightjar. Head is slowly turned, making stripe "snake"

Wryneck's complex patterned plumage is unique. Sky-pointing display is used in courtship or when threatened. Feeds on insects licked up with its long tongue. Nests in tree holes. Undulating flight is woodpecker-like. "Quie-quie" call is heard in spring. Summer visitor (Apr-Sept) to Britain (especially SE England and parts of Scotland), but now rare breeder.

Green Woodpecker

 Nuthatch

Lesser Spotted Woodpecker

Greater Spotted Woodpecker

Predominantly green plumage above with bright crimson crown and striking yellow rump render bird unmistakable. Underparts are greenish yellow below with under-wing
◄ barred pale yellowish. Cp other birds (above)

Alights on tree with upward swoop from flight and moves vertically up trunk, often in a spiral, stopping often to hammer at bark in search of grubs or lick insects up with its tongue ▼

Juv

◄ Juv has a black-streaked pale face, lacking the black area and moustache of adults

♂

Red moustachial stripe of ♂ stands out vividly against the black face. Spiky, stiff tail feathers are used as a support on the trunk and often appear very splayed and worn as a result ►

♂

Contrast of red, black, green and yellow plumage with dark tail stands out vividly on bird taking off ►

Yellow rump

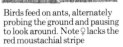

♀

Birds feed on ants, alternately probing the ground and pausing to look around. Note ♀ lacks the red moustachial stripe

Juv is paler above and below with marked streaking on breast

Largest of the British woodpeckers, with plumage colours which prevent confusion with any other bird, although distinctive yellow rump has led to confusion with Golden Oriole. Like all woodpeckers, has extremely long, sticky tongue. *Spends much more time on ground than other woodpeckers,* moving in clumsy hops with frequent surveys of its surroundings. Flight is more deeply undulating than other British woodpeckers, with marked closure of wings between beats. *Call is loud, ringing laugh.* Drums very rarely. Nests high up in trees, excavating own hole (often evicted by Starlings). Favours heathland and open parkland with trees. Resident in all parts of Britain except N Scotland. (No woodpeckers in Ireland.)

Grey-headed Woodpecker

♂ has all-grey head, red eye and red forehead (Green's whole cap is red)

Red cap

Black stripe

♂

◄ Seen from behind in flight, looks identical to Green Woodpecker. Only full view of head will distinguish sp

♀

Wing-barring almost identical to Green Woodpecker

Juv has dull grey head and ► slightly barred underparts with faint black moustache. Profile is dumpier than in Green and juv lacks streaking of juv Green

Juv

◄ Lack of neck in profile is quite unlike Green Woodpecker

Easily confused with Green Woodpecker, both species sharing identical plumage features on rump, wings and tail. *Grey-headed can look much more squat and round-headed when perched. Laughing call, growing slower and deeper as it is uttered,* also distinguishes. Both species often occur together in Europe, but Grey-headed never occurs in British Isles.

Three-toed Woodpecker

Note juv ♂'s yellow ► crown and dark back (cp with adults). Duskier flanks and underparts separate Three-toed sp from other woodpeckers

Juv

Note distribution of white on flying bird, esp on centre of back

Yellow

♀

White

♂

White

♀ has white streaking on top of ► crown, with back of crown jet black and bordered by a white line encircling nape. Black face, bordered by white lines is seen on no other woodpecker. Note small spotting on upperparts

♀

Large-headed, medium-sized woodpecker with three, not four toes. *Yellow on male's head and white mark down centre of adult's back are unique in woodpeckers.* Black face with white streaks delineating reverses normal woodpecker face pattern. Occurs in coniferous forests of N Europe and mountains of S and central Europe. Never found in British Isles.

Great Spotted Woodpecker

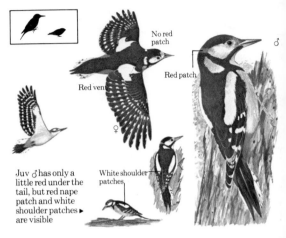

No red patch

Red patch

Red vent

♀

Juv ♂ has only a little red under the tail, but red nape patch and white shoulder patches ▶ are visible

White shoulder patches

Great Spotted is distinguished from Lesser Spotted Woodpecker both in flight and at rest by its *red vent and white shoulders*. Drums loudly in spring and can be located by its tapping. Very undulating flight. Explosive "tchick" call. Common throughout Britain in wooded areas. Few records in Ireland.

Lesser Spotted Woodpecker

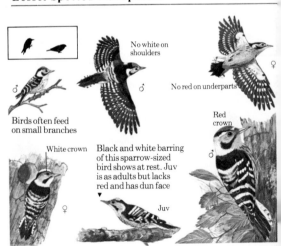

No white on shoulders

♂

No red on underparts

♀

♂

Birds often feed on small branches

White crown

Red crown

♂

Black and white barring of this sparrow-sized bird shows at rest. Juv is as adults but lacks red and has dun face ▼

♀

Juv

Smallest European woodpecker. Lack of red in underparts distinguishes from all other pied woodpeckers. Male has red and female white crown. Typica undulating flight, also moth-like floating display flight. High "qui-qui-qui-qui" call. Found in woods and parks (usually seen on smaller branches than Great Spotted species) in Britain S of Tees.

White-backed Woodpecker

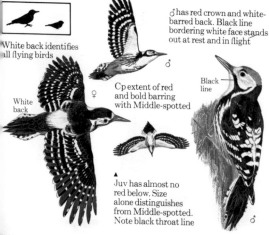

♂ has red crown and white-barred back. Black line bordering white face stands out at rest and in flight

White back identifies all flying birds

♂

Black line

♀

White back

Cp extent of red and bold barring with Middle-spotted

Juv has almost no red below. Size alone distinguishes from Middle-spotted. Note black throat line

♂

Largest of the spotted woodpeckers. Black moustachial stripe continuing down onto breast is diagnostic and *square white patch on rump and back identifies all birds in flight.* Has more white on upper wing than Middle-spotted species. Typical undulating woodpecker flight. Rarest of the European woodpeckers. Never found in British Isles.

Middle Spotted Woodpecker

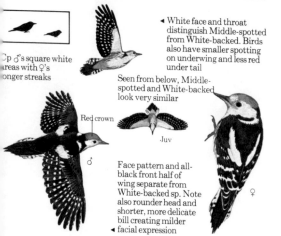

◄ White face and throat distinguish Middle-spotted from White-backed. Birds also have smaller spotting on underwing and less red under tail

Cp ♂'s square white areas with ♀'s longer streaks

Seen from below, Middle-spotted and White-backed look very similar

Red crown

♂

Juv

Face pattern and all-black front half of wing separate from White-backed sp. Note also rounder head and shorter, more delicate bill creating milder ◄ facial expression

♀

Slightly smaller than Great Spotted, but smaller bill and plainer head pattern gives Middle-spotted a very different appearance. *White sides to head make whole head look pale.* Compare neck stripe on flying bird with similar plumage pattern on White-backed. Call is a single, nasal note. Rarely drums. Does not occur in British Isles.

Black Woodpecker

Crow-like dimensions and silhouette are reinforced by jet black plumage. The long spiky tail and the head held well forward show in its undulating flight

Slightly bulbous head on thin neck shows in flight ▼

Splayed wing tip

Birds adopt sky-pointing posture in territorial display ▶

♂'s red crown covers the top of the head completely but is less extensive in the ♀. The red area is often difficult to see in flight ▶

Large pale bill

Pale eye

♂

Nest holes often ▶ look too large for the tree

♀

◀ Shape of head and neck accentuates hammer-headed profile to give an appearance quite unlike any other European woodpecker

Size alone makes this species unmistakable. Its large, pale bill and pale eye together with plumage colours, provide further identification. Rather shy and, although quick to take flight, not as easy to observe as its size might indicate. Tapping for food (main diet is ants) may indicate its presence and spring drumming display is extremely loud. Call is a loud, ringing "chock-chock-chock". Confined to mature beech and conifer woodland on Continent, mainly in E Europe. Generally sedentary (movements of young birds occur), but spreading westwards and nesting in Denmark (probably only reoccupying deforested areas which have grown up again). No records in the British Isles.

Roller

Juv lacks black tip ▶ on outer tail

Steady, buoyant flight is easy to see at a distance, but plumage is not

◀ Rolling display flight shows plumage well

Spring adults

◀ Juv is duller than adults

Jackdaw-sized bird, with large head and bill, and *unmistakable combination of blues and chestnut in spring plumage* (becomes duller in autumn). Easily overlooked in its long periods of sitting quietly. Perches on wires and trees looking out for insect prey on ground. Call is a harsh "krak-krak". Occasional visitor to British Isles (Apr-Oct).

Bee-eater

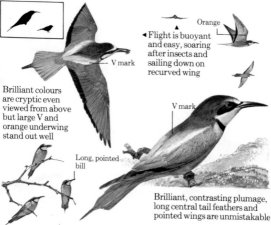

Orange

◀ Flight is buoyant and easy, soaring after insects and sailing down on recurved wing

V mark

Brilliant colours are cryptic even viewed from above but large V and orange underwing stand out well

V mark

Long, pointed bill

Brilliant, contrasting plumage, long central tail feathers and pointed wings are unmistakable

Breathtaking colours, pointed bill and overall shape are unique. Often seen in groups, perching on wires and bare branches. Juvenile is duller than adults, without projecting tail feather. Constant, liquid "quieilp" call and harsher, slurring "churrur-churrur" sound. Has nested but very rare summer visitor to Britain (Apr-Oct).

Hoopoe

Slightly down-curved bill

Crest is raised on landing and in flight

Flight is jerky and bouncing with many changes of direction. Dazzling barred wing pattern, long bill and head shape are unmistakable

Feeding bird is easily overlooked ▶

Raised crest and long tail are unmistakable

Once seen, the Hoopoe cannot be mistaken, but is easily overlooked when busy feeding unobtrusively on tilled fields, and often not seen until it takes flight. Bill is used for digging grubs from ground. Unhygienic nester. *Call is a hollow "poop-oop-oop-oop".* Has nested in Britain. Occurs British Isles Mar-Oct and, rarely, in winter.

Magpie

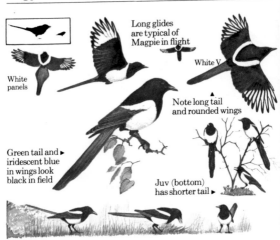

Long glides are typical of Magpie in flight

White V

White panels

Note long tail and rounded wings

Green tail and ▶ iridescent blue in wings look black in field

Juv (bottom) has shorter tail ▶

Shape, plumage, weak-looking flight and harsh, chattering call make Magpie unmistakable. Has a deliberate tail-up walk on ground (also hops). Wary birds found in treetops and hedgerows, usually in pairs but seen in greater numbers in winter. Notorious predator of eggs and young in breeding season. Absent from extreme N Scotland and outlying islands.

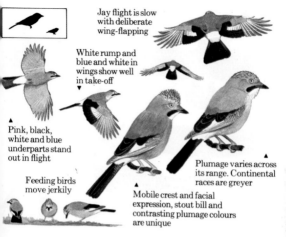

Jay flight is slow with deliberate wing-flapping

White rump and blue and white in wings show well in take-off ▼

Pink, black, white and blue underparts stand out in flight ▲

Feeding birds move jerkily

Mobile crest and facial expression, stout bill and contrasting plumage colours are unique ▲

Plumage varies across its range. Continental races are greyer ▲

Raucous and extremely wary bird. Omnivorous feeder on ground and in trees, and will bury acorns in autumn. Jerky flight between trees, spending little time exposed. *Harsh, screeching call* is part of a wide repertoire. Usually seen in pairs. Found in woodland, parks and large, wooded gardens. Widely distributed S of Aberdeen.

Siberian Jay

Orange underwing

Soft colours contrast with darker head and bill. Flight similar to Jay

Deep orange tail

Grey centre

Bristles show as pale patch on top of bill

Dark head

Grey and orange breast

Note pale grey collar below dark brown cap ▼

Note pouch full of food

Inhabitant of taiga forest of Eurasia and almost unknown outside its range. *Unlike any other European bird; smaller and less aggressive-looking than the Jay with orange-red panels in wing and tail* that draw attention at once. Has "sooc-cooc" call, but is quieter than Jay and much tamer, readily coming to food in winter. No records in British Isles.

Jackdaw

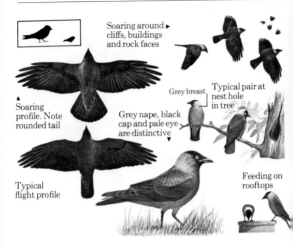

Soaring around ▶ cliffs, buildings and rock faces

▲ Soaring profile. Note rounded tail

Grey breast

Typical pair at nest hole in tree

Grey nape, black cap and pale eye are distinctive ▼

Typical flight profile

Feeding on rooftops

Smallest of the common "crows". Perky and inquisitive, often to be seen strutting on ground and rooftops. May be seen singly but highly gregarious. Nests in buildings, cliff-faces and trees. Flight is hurried looking. *Has ringing "keeack" and "kyaw" calls in its wide vocabulary.* Generally distributed throughout Britain.

Nutcracker

Birds free fall from ▲ highest vantage point, gaining speed for their slow, undulating, Jay-like flight

White triangle

Short tail

Very broad wing

Note heavy spotting on underparts and back ▼

Long "stabber" bill, spotted plumage and dark wing are unique ▼

Pouch under bill for autumn pine-seed collecting

Siberian race's tail

White terminal band

Unique long-billed, Jackdaw-sized crow. Races overlap in their upland conifer-forest habitat, but central European race has thicker bill than Scandinavian race, and thin-billed Siberian race has less white in tail. Call is a high-pitched "caw". Scarce visitor (1-2 per year), usually to S coast, except for irruption in 1968 (more than 300).

Chough

Gliding profile shows up-curved wings (cp Jackdaw)

Square tail (cp Alpine sp)

Ragged look in flight

Curved red bill

Juv has orange bill

Blue-black plumage

Splayed wing tips

Red legs

Jackdaws and Choughs in mixed flocks appear similar from ground

Jackdaw

Most often seen wheeling overhead in large flocks, calling noisily and performing aerobatics. Jackdaw-sized with large, broad, ragged-looking wings. Call is a distinct, sharp, high-pitched "kee-ow". *Red bill and legs distinguish it from other crows* and glossy blue plumage from the blacker-looking Alpine Chough. Inhabits cliffs, quarries and ruins .

Alpine Chough

Cp flatter profile with Chough

Bill shorter than Chough

Alpine sp has a more typical "crow" profile than Chough

Wings narrower than Chough. Tail is longer and more wedge-shaped

Diagnostic yellow bill

Birds feed on scraps near buildings and ski lifts

Alpine sp has rounder head and smaller bill than Chough

Body is plumper and more pear-shaped than Chough, and wing tips fall short of tail

Red legs

At a distance, difficult to distinguish from Chough and Jackdaw, although there are differences in profile and wing shape. Juveniles have blackish legs which change to red in adult. Rolling "skirrish" call. Restricted to high mountain ranges such as Alps and Pyrenees above snow line in summer, but at lower altitudes in winter. No records in Britain.

Carrion Crow

Head shorter than Rook or Raven

Slow, measured flight and all-black plumage identify Crow ▼

Square wings and tail distinguish from Rook and Raven. Tail is rounded when soaring

Cawing bird

◄ Cp Crow's neat leg feathers with the "shaggy trousers" of the Rook

Typical profile in flight

Deep, croaking "kraah" and "kerwark" calls distinguish Crow from Rook, although it may resemble juvenile Rook. Very wary, *usually seen singly or in pairs,* but may form small flocks. Occupies very large urban centres, where Rook is absent. Most *deliberate flight* of all non-predators. Common throughout British Isles apart from Ireland and NW Scotland.

Hooded Crow

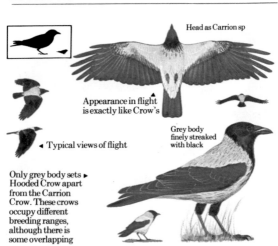

Head as Carrion sp

Appearance in flight is exactly like Crow's

◄ Typical views of flight

Grey body finely streaked with black

Only grey body sets ► Hooded Crow apart from the Carrion Crow. These crows occupy different breeding ranges, although there is some overlapping

Behaviour and habits are exactly the same as Carrion Crow's. Typical crow gait (more deliberate and less waddling than Rook's). *Always nests solitarily* and is territorial. Very subtle distinction between voice of two species. Hooded Crow replaces Carrion in Ireland and NW Scotland. Occasional winter visitor England and Wales, especially on coast.

Rook

Long head

Crow

Wedge tail

Rook

Rook juv

Long bill

Cawing bird

Wings are more pointed than Crow's

High forehead

Bare face

Drooping flanks

Shape in flight and at rest differs from Crow, but *bare face is major distinguishing feature*. Flight in action is faster and more flexible. Gait is more waddling. Rooks are *highly gregarious, colonial nesters*. Prolonged "kaak" call is higher pitched than Crow. Occurs throughout British Isles mainly on agricultural land but also in gardens and towns.

Raven

Soaring birds

Tumbling birds

Wedge shape

Raven has long head and bill, relatively narrow, pointed wings and long, wedged tail

Long thin wing

Note huge bill and shaggy "beard"

Its *huge size (larger than Buzzard)* and easy, soaring flight with regular, powerful wingbeats identify the Raven, which for all its bulk is a great aerial acrobat. *Deep, often repeated "pruk-pruk" and "grok" calls.* Usually seen in pairs, although flocks not uncommon. Occurs in mountain and moorland in W Britain and in Ireland.

Corncrake

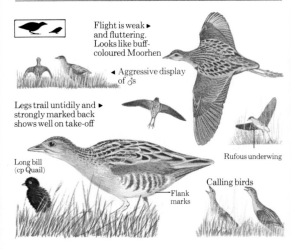

Flight is weak ▶ and fluttering. Looks like buff-coloured Moorhen

◀ Aggressive display of ♂s

Legs trail untidily and ▶ strongly marked back shows well on take-off

Rufous underwing

Long bill (cp Quail)

Flank marks

Calling birds

Skulking, elusive birds that will vanish into the smallest area of cover. *Endless "rack-rack, rack-rack" calling* (like a stick drawn across a comb) locates birds in summer. Preference for hayfields. Still fairly common summer visitor (mid-Apr-Oct) in Ireland and Scottish isles, but very local and patchy elsewhere in Britain.

Quail

Cp Partridge

Head pattern of ♂

Rather like a tiny, young Partridge, with its white-flecked brown upper plumage. Any view of birds is likely to be fleeting ▼

Swift, direct flight with rapid wingbeat differs from Partridge ▼

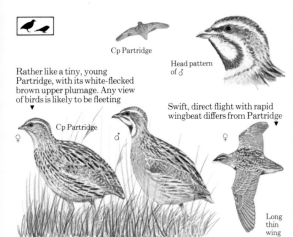

Cp Partridge

♀

♂

♀

Long thin wing

Stubbornly resist most attempts to flush them and are thus very difficult to see. Quails betray presence by emphatic deceptively *ventriloquistic* "quit-ker-hit" call, heard end of May-July. Summer visitor (May-Oct) to corn, hay or rough fields, and some birds winter. Widespread but local in Britain outside Scotland, but numbers vary from year to year.

Partridge

Cream bill

Typical view of
gliding bird ▲

Orange
head

Grey
breast

Maroon
horseshoe

Grey legs

Grey flanks have
reddish-brown marks

Cp wing shape
with Red-legged sp

All partridges look like round
blobs when seen in the field

Note grey breast
and "horseshoe"

Common, usually in pairs or groups, on farmland, heath and moorland. *Orange head, grey breast, barred flanks and "horseshoe"* of adults distinguish from Red-legged species. If disturbed, flies low in loose formation, with several wingbeats and long, bow-winged glides. Fast runner. Grating "krik-ik" call. Resident throughout British Isles (scarce in NW Scotland).

Red-legged Partridge

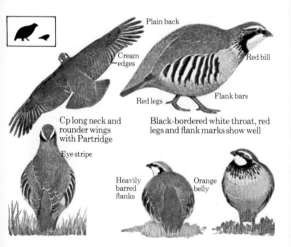

Plain back

Cream
edges

Red bill

Flank bars

Red legs

Cp long neck and
rounder wings
with Partridge

Black-bordered white throat, red
legs and flank marks show well

Eye stripe

Heavily
barred
flanks

Orange
belly

Generally rounder in shape, more inclined to run than fly and more often seen on bare open ground than Partridge. *Often seen on roofs and fences.* (Partridge never perch.) Two species frequently occur together, and flight is very similar. Call harsh "chuck-chuck-chuckor" and measured "check-check". Resident in Britain (principally S and E England).

Pheasant

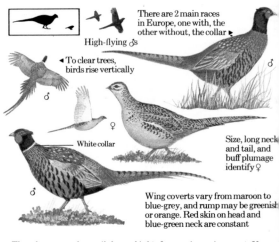

There are 2 main races in Europe, one with, the other without, the collar ►

High-flying ♂s

◄ To clear trees, birds rise vertically

♂

♀

White collar

♂

Size, long neck and tail, and buff plumage identify ♀

Wing coverts vary from maroon to blue-grey, and rump may be greenish or orange. Red skin on head and blue-green neck are constant

The only common, long-tailed game bird (a few exotic species occur). Young may look like lanky, spike-tailed Partridge before tail has grown. Flight is usually short and low (except on shoots), with flaps and long glides. If disturbed, rises with shocking clatter and echoing double crow. Common resident throughout British Isles except W and N Scotland.

Hazelhen

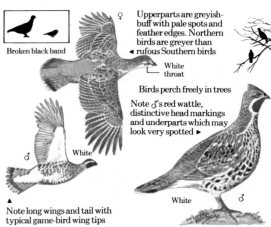

Broken black band

♀

Upperparts are greyish-buff with pale spots and feather edges. Northern birds are greyer than ◄ rufous Southern birds

White throat

Birds perch freely in trees

Note ♂'s red wattle, distinctive head markings and underparts which may look very spotted ►

♂

White

▲
Note long wings and tail with typical game-bird wing tips

White

♂

Only small European woodland grouse, and a species very much at home in trees. Plumage, body shape and voice are unusual and distinguish it from other game birds. *Dark tail band shows well* in bird going away. Wings hiss in flight. Rather high whistling call. Sedentary species occurring in mixed woodland in parts of Europe. No records in British Isles.

Capercaillie

Extremely noisy when taking off from trees but silent in flight, which is swift and strong, with series of flaps followed by a tilting glide

♀

Adult ♂s in flight

♀

♀s have buff above with rufous tail. Note white underwing patches

♀

Orange breast band

♀

Splayed wing tips (typical of all game birds)

Adult ♂ in display

Birds raise crown and swell throat if anxious. Note rufous tail and flank marks

♂ puffed up in display. Note two white spots

Size (*male is almost as large as a turkey*) prevents confusion with other species. Young males have shorter tails and show an odd mixture of plumage. *Species is confined to coniferous forests.* In summer female and young feed on the ground and in autumn may be found in stubble fields or even heather, some way from woodland. Males feed on pine shoots in trees. Birds roost in trees at night. Males are extremely territorial in spring and have an elaborate courtship display, which is accompanied by an extraordinary cacophony of calls and intermittent leaps into the air, noisily flapping wings. Resident in Scotland N of Firth of Forth and recently reintroduced in the Lake District. Absent from Ireland.

Red Grouse/Willow Grouse

Note head-up pot-bellied profile

White contrasts with dark plumage on flying bird ▼

Partridge-shaped bird distinguished by dark red-brown plumage with brown flight feathers and tail

Rounded tail

♀ and imm Red Grouse are less red than ♂, with more buff plumage above and below. Both sexes have bright red patches over the eye and whitish legs in all plumages

Widespread primaries ►

Spring ♂   Spring ♀

Spring ♂ is distinguished from ♀ and imm by richer red plumage

Willow Grouse (Norwegian race)

Willow Grouse (autumn)

Willow Grouse (winter)

Willow Grouse (summer)

Spring ♂

Flying bird in summer and autumn is like Red Grouse with pure white wings. Heavier bill separates pure-white winter bird from very similar Ptarmigan. Coastal Norwegian race has red flanks in summer

Red Grouse is the familiar moorland game bird. Slightly larger than the Partridge with a similar plump, broad-winged profile in flight. Despite slight plumage variations *bird usually looks very dark,* almost soot-coloured at times. Two species are identical in size and behaviour and only distinguished by different plumage and distribution. Flight is rapid and low over ground, as series of fast wingbeats followed by rocking glide. Usually calls when flushed. *Red Grouse gives guttural "kow-kok-ok-ok-ok"* Also has distinctive deep "go-bak" call. Red Grouse is confined to British Isles but absent S of a line from Severn to Humber. Willow Grouse is confined to N Europe and never occurs in British Isles.

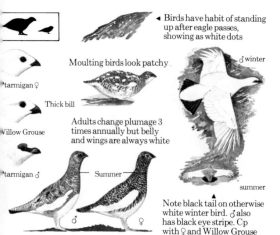

◄ Birds have habit of standing up after eagle passes, showing as white dots

Moulting birds look patchy

♂ winter

Ptarmigan ♀

Thick bill

Willow Grouse

Adults change plumage 3 times annually but belly and wings are always white

Ptarmigan ♂ — Summer —

♂   ♀

summer

▲
Note black tail on otherwise white winter bird. ♂ also has black eye stripe. Cp with ♀ and Willow Grouse

smaller than Grouse but similar in shape and appearance in flight. Extremely tame, but very difficult to pick out in its mountain-top and rocky hillside habitat. *More delicate bill distinguishes males from similarly patterned Willow Grouse.* Call is croaking rattling "arrrrrruk". Resident and sedentary in Scotland.

Black Grouse Ⓡ

♂

Forked tail

Adult ♀

White bar

Lyre-shaped tail

Larger and greyer than Red sp. Cp wing shape

Colour contrast on ♂ taking off

♀ plumage is a rich reddish brown with 2 pale wing-bars

♂ and ♀ have pure white underwing

♀

Breeding ♂

Tail is spread, wings drooped and combs raised in display

Tail shape, which differs in male and female, and *black and white male plumage* distinguish Black Grouse from other game birds. Immature male in eclipse plumage is not jet black. Spectacular group courtship display. Flight is fast, with rapid wingbeats and long glides. Found in forest or forest fringes, heath and moorland in Britain W of line Humber-Severn.

Cuckoo

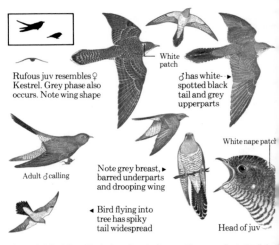

Rufous juv resembles ♀ Kestrel. Grey phase also occurs. Note wing shape

White patch

♂ has white-spotted black tail and grey upperparts

Adult ♂ calling

Note grey breast, ► barred underparts and drooping wing

◄ Bird flying into tree has spiky tail widespread

White nape patch

Head of juv

Superficially falcon-like in its pointed wings and long, graduated tail, but *small, pointed head held high,* and bill shape distinguish. Adult and first summer female have buff on breast. Level, lowish flight with shallow wingbeats. Only male gives "cuckoo" call and also has scolding, growling calls. Female has liquid, bubbling call. Common summer visitor.

Nightjar

White spots (♂ only)

♂ Barred underwing   Typical flight profiles

Birds perch flat along branch

Bars on wings and body

White in tail (♂ only)

Bristles save eyes from insect damage

Nesting bird

Cryptic plumage pattern and enormous gape make Nightjar unique. Buoyant flight on long, angled wings will identify flying bird. May be seen hunting at dusk, bounding and twisting to catch moths. Loud "churring" song. Nests on suitable heathland and young plantations throughout British Isles, but decreasing. Summer visitor (end Apr–Sept).

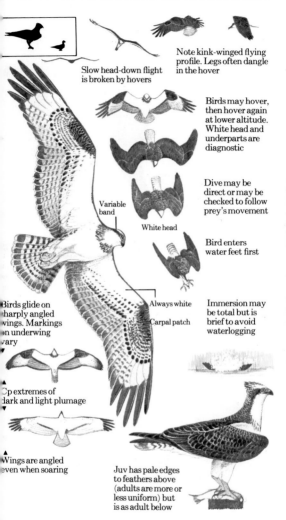

Note kink-winged flying profile. Legs often dangle in the hover

Slow head-down flight is broken by hovers

Birds may hover, then hover again at lower altitude. White head and underparts are diagnostic

Dive may be direct or may be checked to follow prey's movement

Variable band

White head

Bird enters water feet first

Birds glide on sharply angled wings. Markings on underwing vary

Always white

Carpal patch

Immersion may be total but is brief to avoid waterlogging

Cp extremes of dark and light plumage

Wings are angled even when soaring

Juv has pale edges to feathers above (adults are more or less uniform) but is as adult below

Large brown and white bird of prey with disproportionately long, narrow wings which are kinked when seen from front or rear and angled when seen from below. *White head and dark brown eye stripe are always conspicuous.* Prominent brown to pale breast band is usually present. Underwing varies from very pale to greyish brown. Always associated with water but may nest some distance from water's edge, often roosting or taking prey to site well away from water. Breeds in Scotland (Apr-Sept), but also a passage migrant seen around lakes, reservoirs and coast (Apr-May and Aug-Sept) sometimes remaining in area for some days. Wide global distribution but numbers in Europe affected by persecution and water pollution.

Kestrel

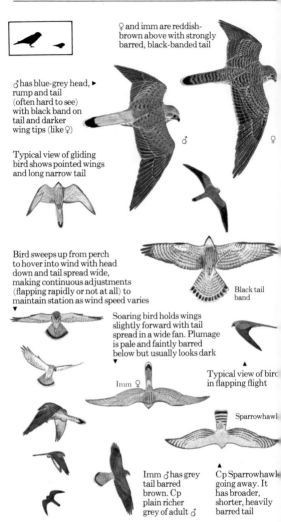

♀ and imm are reddish-brown above with strongly barred, black-banded tail

♂ has blue-grey head, ▶ rump and tail (often hard to see) with black band on tail and darker wing tips (like ♀)

Typical view of gliding bird shows pointed wings and long narrow tail

Bird sweeps up from perch to hover into wind with head down and tail spread wide, making continuous adjustments (flapping rapidly or not at all) to maintain station as wind speed varies

Black tail band

Soaring bird holds wings slightly forward with tail spread in a wide fan. Plumage is pale and faintly barred below but usually looks dark

Imm ♀

Typical view of bird in flapping flight

Sparrowhawk

Imm ♂ has grey tail barred brown. Cp plain richer grey of adult ♂

Cp Sparrowhawk going away. It has broader, shorter, heavily barred tail

Commonest bird of prey occurring everywhere throughout the British Isles from city centres to bleak moorland. *Probably most frequently seen hovering above motorway verges.* Where they occur together, it is sometimes confused with Hobby, Merlin or Sparrowhawk, but it is *distinguished by the long tail and the habit of continuous hovering.* May be seen perching on trees, buildings, and power lines. Feeds principally on voles but will take small birds and large insects. Nests in buildings, trees or suitable nest boxes. Typical falcon flight —a series of flaps interspersed with glides. Frequently soars. "Slides" down steeply to take prey from hover. High-pitched "qui-qui-qui" call. Resident but also winter visitor.

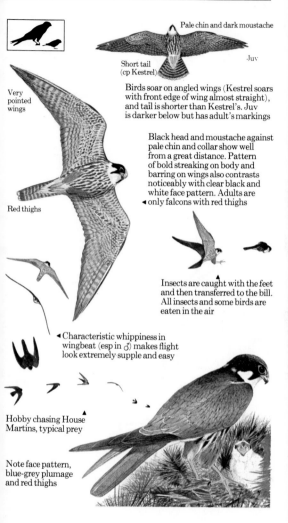

Pale chin and dark moustache

Short tail (cp Kestrel)

Juv

Birds soar on angled wings (Kestrel soars with front edge of wing almost straight), and tail is shorter than Kestrel's. Juv is darker below but has adult's markings

Very pointed wings

Black head and moustache against pale chin and collar show well from a great distance. Pattern of bold streaking on body and barring on wings also contrasts noticeably with clear black and white face pattern. Adults are ◄ only falcons with red thighs

Red thighs

Insects are caught with the feet and then transferred to the bill. All insects and some birds are eaten in the air

◄ Characteristic whippiness in wingbeat (esp in ♂) makes flight look extremely supple and easy

Hobby chasing House Martins, typical prey

Note face pattern, blue-grey plumage and red thighs

Slim, elegant, handsomely plumaged bird which *may look like a huge swift at a distance. Head pattern identifies all birds.* Female and smaller male have same plumage. Juv has dark, brownish upperparts. Often shows regularity in feeding like other predators, appearing same time and place each day. Mercurial in flight, can be overhead and then far distant in a trice. Superb skill on wing enables it to catch other consummate fliers such as swifts, and birds may be taken without any faltering in flight. Hobby calls only in breeding season. Rare breeder (under 100 pairs) in Britain, frequenting heathland and wooded agricultural land, mainly S of Wash. Summer visitor (Apr/May-Oct).

Sparrowhawk

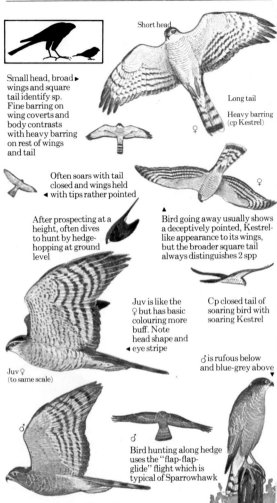

Short head

Long tail

Heavy barring
(cp Kestrel)

Small head, broad ►
wings and square
tail identify sp.
Fine barring on
wing coverts and
body contrasts
with heavy barring
on rest of wings
and tail

♀

Often soars with tail
closed and wings held
◄ with tips rather pointed

♀

After prospecting at a
height, often dives
to hunt by hedge-
hopping at ground
level

Bird going away usually shows
a deceptively pointed, Kestrel-
like appearance to its wings,
but the broader square tail
always distinguishes 2 spp

Juv is like the
♀ but has basic
colouring more
buff. Note
head shape and
◄ eye stripe

Cp closed tail of
soaring bird with
soaring Kestrel

Juv ♀
(to same scale)

♂ is rufous below
and blue-grey above
▼

♂

Bird hunting along hedge
uses the "flap-flap-
glide" flight which is
typical of Sparrowhawk

Small size makes it the most agile of woodland predators, able to dash in
and out of trees in pursuit of small birds. *Females are grey-brown above and
white-barred below. The smaller male is identifiable by its blue-grey upperparts
and very rich rufous underparts.* Juvenile male and female are identical.
Feeds exclusively on birds caught on wing or taken from ground. Male
mainly takes sparrows and tits, but female preys on larger birds such as
thrushes and Starlings. Has slow soaring flight (especially seen in Mar-
Apr) as part of display. Resident and widespread throughout British Isles
wherever there is suitable cover (including urban gardens) and population
now recovering from decline due to pesticide poisoning.

Goshawk

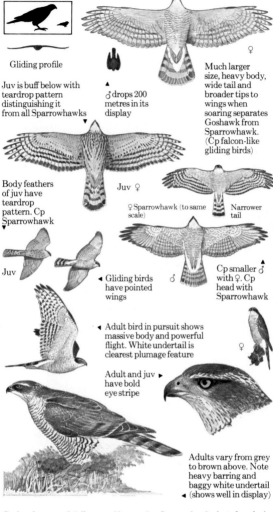

Gliding profile

Juv is buff below with teardrop pattern distinguishing it from all Sparrowhawks

♂ drops 200 metres in its display

♀

Much larger size, heavy body, wide tail and broader tips to wings when soaring separates Goshawk from Sparrowhawk. (Cp falcon-like gliding birds)

Body feathers of juv have teardrop pattern. Cp Sparrowhawk

Juv ♀

♀ Sparrowhawk (to same scale)

Narrower tail

Juv

Gliding birds have pointed wings

♂

Cp smaller ♂ with ♀. Cp head with Sparrowhawk

Adult bird in pursuit shows massive body and powerful flight. White undertail is clearest plumage feature

♀

Adult and juv ► have bold eye stripe

Adults vary from grey to brown above. Note heavy barring and baggy white undertail ◄ (shows well in display)

Goshawks *superficially resemble massive Sparrowhawks* but female is Buzzard-sized bird and both adults give an immediate impression of muscular power with their easy wingbeats in flight. *Triangular head, broad, very solid-looking body and wide base to tail* will always distinguish Goshawks. *White undertail coverts show at a great distance, especially when soaring* (which may be followed by plummet), in male's spring display. Freshly moulted adults have blue-grey plumage which fades to brown. Quiet, easily overlooked bird of suitable woodland, which takes mainly rabbits and Wood Pigeons, with dashing Sparrowhawk-like flight in pursuit. Rare but regular breeder in Britain and probably increasing.

Peregrine

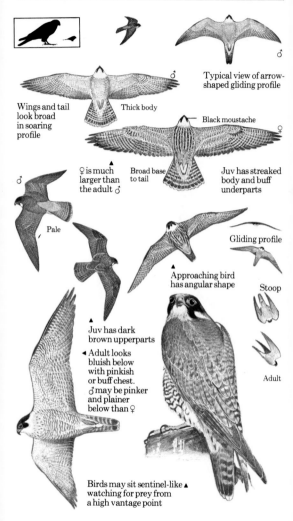

Typical view of arrow-shaped gliding profile

Wings and tail look broad in soaring profile

Thick body

Black moustache

♀ is much larger than the adult ♂

Broad base to tail

Juv has streaked body and buff underparts

Pale

Gliding profile

Approaching bird has angular shape

Stoop

Juv has dark brown upperparts

◄ Adult looks bluish below with pinkish or buff chest. ♂ may be pinker and plainer below than ♀

Adult

Birds may sit sentinel-like ▲ watching for prey from a high vantage point

Largest resident falcon in the British Isles and a magnificently powerful and fast flier. Very heavily built (female is much larger), with a rather angular shape and broad base to tail. Presence frequently betrayed by all birds taking wing in a general panic. Flight is series of fast, "winnowing" wingbeats followed by a glide. Often soars but does not hover. Takes birds in the air, either diving in a spectacular near-vertical stoop and bowling its prey out of the sky, or following in a direct chase. Nests in inaccessible places, favouring sea cliffs in British Isles, although also breeds inland. Global in its range but population only recently recovering from sharp decline. Movement from inland areas to coast from Aug onwards.

Merlin

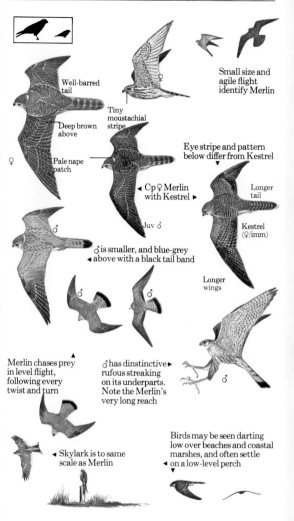

Small size and agile flight identify Merlin

Well-barred tail

Deep brown above

Tiny moustachial stripe

Pale nape patch

♀

Eye stripe and pattern below differ from Kestrel

◀ Cp ♀ Merlin with Kestrel ▶

Longer tail

Kestrel (♀/imm)

Juv ♂

♂

♂ is smaller, and blue-grey above with a black tail band

Longer wings

♂

♂

Merlin chases prey in level flight, following every twist and turn

♂ has dinstinctive ▶ rufous streaking on its underparts. Note the Merlin's very long reach

♂

◀ Skylark is to same scale as Merlin

Birds may be seen darting low over beaches and coastal marshes, and often settle ◀ on a low-level perch

Smallest European falcon. Follows every twist and turn of quarry in swift, dashing flight. Sometimes confused with the longer-winged Kestrel but *male's blue-grey plumage is distinctive* and, although female and juvenile look more or less dark brown, the broad-based, *sharply pointed wings, bullet-shaped head and ample tail* give a characteristic silhouette. Only perches on low vantage points. Feeds mainly on small birds such as larks, pipits and waders. Breeds in moorland areas, nesting on ground or in trees. A scarce British Isles resident found W of line from Scarborough to Torquay. Declining as a breeding bird. Some birds winter in lowlands or coastal areas.

101

Marsh Harrier

Imm 1st summer   Pale head   Wing mark

Broad wings
(cp other harriers)

Juv

Adult ♂

Adult ♀

Head shows
up as pale
"beacon" at
◀ a distance

Adult ♀

♂

Juv

Adult ♂ plumage
can be much duller
than this, but
pattern is constant ▶

Adult ♂

Adult ♀

Adult ♂ may be whitish
or patterned below ▼

Adult ♀ is dark "chocolate"
brown with cream head

♂

Typical view of birds
hunting. Flight is
low, slow and flapping
with frequent glides ▼

Largest and most heavily built of the harriers, its size and shape alone distinguishing it from other harrier species. Plumage is variable but the pattern remains constant. Adult males have pale grey wings and tail gradually acquired over three or four years; females and juveniles have dark eye stripe and yellowish head. Feeds on small amphibians, mammals and birds. Has typical slow harrier flight with V-shaped gliding attitude and occasional leg trailing. Shrill call not unlike Buzzard. Resident but breeds irregularly, always nesting in extensive Phragmites reed beds. Passage birds occur in many places in spring and autumn, with some wintering in marshy and coastal areas.

Hen Harrier

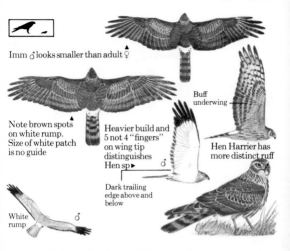

Imm ♂ looks smaller than adult ♀

Note brown spots on white rump. Size of white patch is no guide

Heavier build and 5 not 4 "fingers" on wing tip distinguishes Hen sp ▶

Buff underwing

Hen Harrier has more distinct ruff

Dark trailing edge above and below

White rump ♂

Rump and trailing edge of wing distinguish male from other harriers. Female and juvenile male may be confused with female Montagu's but for their heavier build and more defined patterning below. Typical harrier flight. Breeds in moorland and young conifer but rare in England S of Wash, except as passage and winter visitor (Aug-Apr) to coasts.

Montagu's Harrier

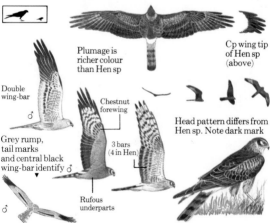

Double wing-bar ♂

Plumage is richer colour than Hen sp

Cp wing tip of Hen sp (above)

Chestnut forewing

Head pattern differs from Hen sp. Note dark mark

Grey rump, tail marks and central black wing-bar identify ♂ ▼

3 bars (4 in Hen)

Rufous underparts

♂

Much more slightly built than Hen Harrier with narrower wings. High in air looks more like a large Kestrel than a harrier. Juvenile unlike Hen, is brick red below (cp Pallid Harrier). Habits similar to Hen Harrier. Nests on heath, young conifer plantations and marsh fringes. Erratically distributed resident and a rare breeder. Also summer visitor (Apr-Sept).

Buzzard

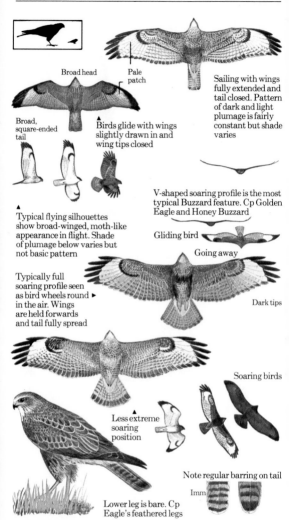

Broad head

Pale patch

Sailing with wings fully extended and tail closed. Pattern of dark and light plumage is fairly constant but shade varies

Broad, square-ended tail

▲ Birds glide with wings slightly drawn in and wing tips closed

▲ Typical flying silhouettes show broad-winged, moth-like appearance in flight. Shade of plumage below varies but not basic pattern

V-shaped soaring profile is the most typical Buzzard feature. Cp Golden Eagle and Honey Buzzard

Gliding bird

Going away

Typically full soaring profile seen as bird wheels round ► in the air. Wings are held forwards and tail fully spread

Dark tips

Soaring birds

▲ Less extreme soaring position

Lower leg is bare. Cp Eagle's feathered legs

Note regular barring on tail

Imm

Usually seen circling at some height, appearing as fairly dark, broad-winged bird, but plumage varies considerably below, from white to chocolate brown (latter is more common in Britain). May be seen in some numbers wheeling over woodland or open country. Birds prey on rabbits, small mammals such as mice, and earthworms and beetles. Normal flight is direct with powerful, regular wingbeats, but often interspersed with glides. *Call is a frequently uttered high "whee-eur".* Prefers mixed wood and agricultural land but may often occur on upland and moorland. Resident in Britain, though very local in eastern half of England. Also occurs in northern tip of Ireland but virtually absent farther south.

Profile of bird soaring, gliding or sailing

Long thin tail

Pale form gliding with tail closed. Plumage colour varies greatly, but pattern of barring is same (note tail esp)

◄ Soaring bird may look very Buzzard-like, but wings are less "shapely", tail less rounded and head shape different

Note adult's pale eye

Long head

Cp pattern of barring on wings and tail with Buzzard

◄ Soaring birds

Juv has dark eye

Small pigeon-like head may show well in flight at certain angles. Appearance is surprisingly mild for a predator ▼

Honey Buzzard has 2 or 3 prominent bars against a background of fainter bars. Cp with Buzzard's more uniform barring

Plumage variations can make Honey Buzzard difficult to distinguish from Buzzard, which is similar in size and general shape. Birds may vary from white head and underparts through all shades to chocolate brown overall. *Best identification features are head shape and tail. Diagnostic barring is* continued on wings but clearer on tail. Eats larvae, grubs, wasps and bees, but may supplement diet with small mammals and reptiles. Has flat-winged sailing flight (compare V-winged Buzzard profile). Also has continuous flapping flight when on passage, unlike Buzzard. Soars mainly in display flight. Rare breeder in England and Scotland (May-Sept). Passage birds (numerous in S Europe) may occur May-Sept.

Rough-legged Buzzard

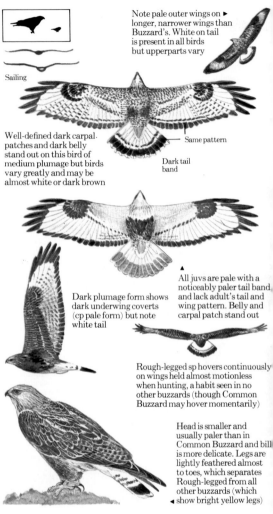

Note pale outer wings on ▶ longer, narrower wings than Buzzard's. White on tail is present in all birds but upperparts vary

Sailing

Well-defined dark carpal patches and dark belly stand out on this bird of medium plumage but birds vary greatly and may be almost white or dark brown

Same pattern

Dark tail band

All juvs are pale with a noticeably paler tail band and lack adult's tail and wing pattern. Belly and carpal patch stand out

Dark plumage form shows dark underwing coverts (cp pale form) but note white tail

Rough-legged sp hovers continuously on wings held almost motionless when hunting, a habit seen in no other buzzards (though Common Buzzard may hover momentarily)

Head is smaller and usually paler than in Common Buzzard and bill is more delicate. Legs are lightly feathered almost to toes, which separates Rough-legged from all other buzzards (which ◀ show bright yellow legs)

Larger than Common Buzzard with narrower wings. Two species are often confused because each shows a great range of plumage pattern. *Dark pattern on white tail and presence of dark belly and carpal patch are diagnostic.* Head and bill is smaller than in Common Buzzard. Juveniles are always paler than adult birds. Occurs principally on heath and open coastal grasslands, but also hunts over agricultural land in winter. Feeds mainly on mice and rabbits. Flight is noticeably less laboured than in Common Buzzard, and *Rough-legged species shows a different angling of the wings in sailing flight.* Winter visitor (Oct-Apr), especially to E coast of Britain. Rare in Ireland. Much commoner in Britain in some years than others.

Black Kite

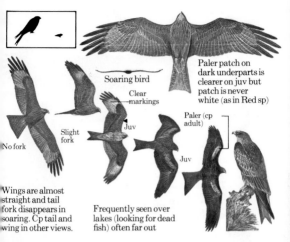

Paler patch on dark underparts is clearer on juv but patch is never white (as in Red sp)

Soaring bird

Clear markings

Juv

Slight fork

No fork

Paler (cp adult)

Juv

Wings are almost straight and tail fork disappears in soaring. Cp tail and wing in other views.

Frequently seen over lakes (looking for dead fish) often far out

Opportunist scavenger and predator of open country and urban areas. *Looks very dark in field with long, thin, angled wings and long, forked or triangular tail.* Tail is very mobile and often twisted in flight. Undulating, veering flight with flapping and glides. Rare migrant (usually May) to E coast of England and Scotland.

Red Kite

Wings very angled

Black wing tips

Wings look long and slender from afar

Tail is very orange. Above, shows pale patch on forewing

Pale head

White patch

Well-forked orange tail is obvious above and below. White wing patch also shows well.

Larger, more rakish build than Black Kite, with much more distinct fork in closed tail and large white wing patches. Colour as well as shape of tail distinguishes (Black Kite's is always brown). Easy flight action, gliding and soaring well using tail as rudder. Breeds in Wales but susceptible to disturbance. Rare elsewhere; a few winter and passage birds.

107

Golden Eagle

Cp shape, size, and pattern on wing of Buzzard

Buzzard

Same scale

Juv

Pale barring

Thick band

◀ White in wing and tail of imm birds gradually disappears

Cp Eagle and Buzzard soaring

Buzzard

Juv

Typical view of receding bird ▼

Buzzard

Pale head

White socks

Pale patches on sub-adult

A few powerful wing-beats are followed by lengthy glides. Drops vertically when diving ▼

Diving

Sometimes drops wings below body (without loss of height when gliding)

Juv gliding

Adults in high wind, gliding

♀ is much larger than ♂

Long tail

♀

Feathered "trousers" distinguish bird from Buzzard and sea eagles

Juv in flight

Largest and most powerful of the true eagles and a magnificent and highly accomplished flier. Most often seen against skyline following ridge, but also may be seen soaring overhead. Occupies huge territories, but four or five birds may be seen together in winter. Food is varied, including birds (sometimes taken in the air), hares and carrion. Flight is powerful, deliberate and easy. Sails and glides a great deal. When quartering flies low, merging into background, only seen when it breaks the skyline. Folds wings and plummets if prey is sighted. Breeds (Mar-Jun) in Scotland and N England but is very rare outside its range. Consistent illegal persecution still affects population.

White-tailed Eagle

Imm 2-3 years old

Pale head held well forward

Large yellow feet

...ure white tail is always ...istinctive, but shape of tail ...aries between individuals and ...ay be almost square ended

Widespread primaries

Wedge shape

...liding profile

Juv is very dark below although tail may have pale flecks. Note almost oblong wings

Rectangular wing shape gives bird in flight a vulture-like appearance

...uge, deep ...ll (cp ...olden sp)

Typical view is of strong, regular beats of huge wings and small head and tail

Huge wings and drooping ▶ head distinguish bird from any other predator

Juv has patchy appearance and is much darker than adult. Note dumpy profile on ground and unfeathered legs ▼

...hort tail ...p Golden ...agle)

...gs unfeathered ...p Golden Eagle)

Juv

Typical sea eagle bill

...argest of the sea eagles. *Rectangular wings dominating flight profile ...stinguish all White-tailed Sea Eagles, even from great range.* Adult birds are ...sily identifiable by white tail and generally pale appearance. ...nfeathered legs will identify all birds at rest. Sluggish in its general habits. ...eeds on large fish and may take sea birds in flight or from the water. Also ...eds on carrion. Often pursued by other birds. Once bred in Scotland and ...w reintroduction is being attempted on a Scottish Island. Otherwise ...ccurs as a rare winter visitor which may appear round British coasts. May ...crease if use of pesticides and continued persecution in its northern ...unts are controlled.

109

Birds of Prey

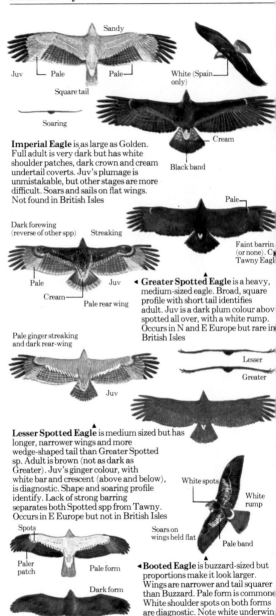

Sandy

Juv — Pale — Pale —

Square tail

Soaring

White (Spain only)

Cream

Black band

Imperial Eagle is as large as Golden. Full adult is very dark but has white shoulder patches, dark crown and cream undertail coverts. Juv's plumage is unmistakable, but other stages are more difficult. Soars and sails on flat wings. Not found in British Isles

Dark forewing (reverse of other spp)   Streaking

Pale

Faint barring (or none). Cf Tawny Eagl

Pale   Juv

Cream

Pale rear wing

◄ **Greater Spotted Eagle** is a heavy, medium-sized eagle. Broad, square profile with short tail identifies adult. Juv is a dark plum colour abov spotted all over, with a white rump. Occurs in N and E Europe but rare in British Isles

Pale ginger streaking and dark rear-wing

Lesser

Greater

Juv

Lesser Spotted Eagle is medium sized but has longer, narrower wings and more wedge-shaped tail than Greater Spotted sp. Adult is brown (not as dark as Greater). Juv's ginger colour, with white bar and crescent (above and below), is diagnostic. Shape and soaring profile identify. Lack of strong barring separates both Spotted spp from Tawny. Occurs in E Europe but not in British Isles

White spots

White rump

Spots

Soars on wings held flat

Pale band

Paler patch   Pale form

Dark form

Square tail

◄ **Booted Eagle** is buzzard-sized but proportions make it look larger. Wings are narrower and tail squarer than Buzzard. Pale form is commone White shoulder spots on both forms are diagnostic. Note white underwin and dark flight feathers. Does not occur in British Isles

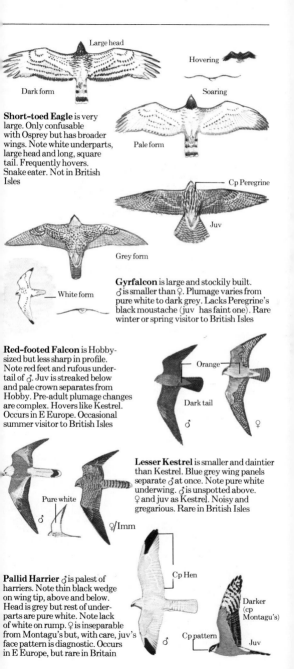

Short-toed Eagle is very large. Only confusable with Osprey but has broader wings. Note white underparts, large head and long, square tail. Frequently hovers. Snake eater. Not in British Isles

Large head

Hovering

Soaring

Dark form

Pale form

Cp Peregrine

Juv

Grey form

White form

Gyrfalcon is large and stockily built. ♂ is smaller than ♀. Plumage varies from pure white to dark grey. Lacks Peregrine's black moustache (juv has faint one). Rare winter or spring visitor to British Isles

Red-footed Falcon is Hobby-sized but less sharp in profile. Note red feet and rufous under-tail of ♂. Juv is streaked below and pale crown separates from Hobby. Pre-adult plumage changes are complex. Hovers like Kestrel. Occurs in E Europe. Occasional summer visitor to British Isles

Orange

Dark tail

♂

♀

Lesser Kestrel is smaller and daintier than Kestrel. Blue grey wing panels separate ♂ at once. Note pure white underwing. ♂ is unspotted above. ♀ and juv as Kestrel. Noisy and gregarious. Rare in British Isles

Pure white

♂

♀/Imm

Pallid Harrier ♂ is palest of harriers. Note thin black wedge on wing tip, above and below. Head is grey but rest of under-parts are pure white. Note lack of white on rump. ♀ is inseparable from Montagu's but, with care, juv's face pattern is diagnostic. Occurs in E Europe, but rare in Britain

Cp Hen

Darker (cp Montagu's)

Cp pattern

Juv

♂

111

British Owls

Most owls are nocturnal and especially active at dawn and dusk, though some (eg Short-eared) may be seen during day. All feed primarily on rodents. Owls need protection; but note that all young leave nest in woolly stage (especially Tawny) and must be left alone—the adults will continue to feed them. All owls on these two pages occur in British Isles and are drawn to same scale.

Scops Owl is a tiny, slim, grey, "eared" owl. Its small head is quite unlike flat "box" of Little Owl. Often occurs in urban areas where persistent "kew" call betrays presence. Birds may be killed on roads, esp where lights attract insects. Summer visitor north to Brittany. Rare vagrant to British Isles

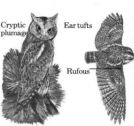

Cryptic plumage

Ear tufts

Rufous

Fine spotting

White eyebrow

White spots

Barred tail

Little Owl is small, squat, and flat-headed. Note round yellow eyes, streaked underparts and heavy spotting above. Often seen in daylight (perched on post and poles). Very undulating, woodpecker like flight. Distinct, plaintive "kiew" call. Resident in Britain. (Very scarce Scotland)

Tawny Owl is best known British Owl, always associated with trees. Large head, round facial disc and large, dark eye identifies. Upperparts are well marked. Most British birds are rufous but grey form also occurs. Nocturnal, mostly seen at dawn and dusk. Emphatic "kee-wick" call and drawn-out hooting. Resident throughout Britain (including cities). Not in Ireland

Characteristic profile

Grey form

White marks (most birds)

Broad round wings

Barn Owl is only common sp with pure white wings below. Usually appears ghostly white in headlights. Face and body of British birds are mainly white but continental birds are buff below (as upperparts). Often seen in daylight when feeding young. Nests in old trees and buildings. Has wavering quartering flight on rather long, narrow wings over open ground. Loud shrieking call. Resident in British Isles

Long legs

Variable upperparts (sometimes very pale)

No white

Tail longer than Short-eared (cp barring)

Long-eared Owl has long ear tufts and orange-yellow eyes. Seen in daylight in winter and when feeding young. Finely barred rear half of wing separates from Short-eared. Deep wing-beats in flight. Low "oo-oo-ooh" call. Resident in British Isles (nests in conifers). Also winter visitor

Cp barring on Short-eared

Dark patch

Short-eared Owl is a patchy-looking, buff-coloured owl. More diurnal than other spp, may be seen hunting low over moorland or marshes. Flight is wavering with glides on noticeably long, crooked wings. Resident (but rare nester in S England). More widely distributed as a winter visitor

White

Patch

European Owls

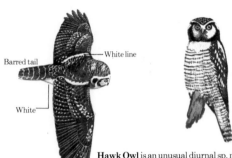

Barred tail

White line

White

Hawk Owl is an unusual diurnal sp, more hawk than owl in body and wing shape, but with large, flat-topped head and yellow eyes. Only European owl with barring on breast (boldness of barring varies). May be seen perching in exposed position, often flicking tail. Hawk-like flight. Chattering call. Occurs in Scandinavian conifer forests. Rare visitor to British Isles

White eyebrows

Dark face

Streaking

Juv

Pigmy Owl is tiny (hardly longer than Great Tit upon which it may prey). Upperparts are brown with tiny white spots. Note yellow eyes and white eyebrows. Frequently seen during daylight. Perches prominently and often raises or jerks tail upwards. Is highly vocal with a shrill "pheeoo" call. Resident in continental mountains but not found in British Isles

Chocolate-brown

Cp head of Little sp

Juv

Cp barring of Little sp

Tengmalm's Owl is slightly larger than Little Owl and superficially resembles it, but has rounded head with facial disc like Tawny. Highly nocturnal sp (but seen in daylight in longest summer days). Flight is wavering (cp undulating flight of Little Owl). Call is a rapid, repeated "coo-coo-coo-coo". Occurs in conifer forest of Central and N Europe. Rare visitor to British Isles

Separate primaries (cp
Barn Owl)

Snowy Owl is huge (♀ is larger than ♂). ♂ is
all-white or has minimal barring, ♀ is heavily
barred and both sexes have white underwings. Yellow
eyes stand out well. Note dense feathering on
feet. May be seen perching on vantage point such
as rock or post. Flight is low with frequent
glides. Silent outside breeding season. Arctic
species, also winter visitor to British
Isles (has bred in Shetland)

Cp elongated
form with Tawny

Dark
eye

Bold
streaking

Line

Strong
barring

Long
barred
tail

Ural Owl is a large grey-brown owl with
round facial disc and round, dark eyes,
but is smaller than Great Grey (cp Snowy,
Ural, Great Grey and Eagle flying, all to
same scale). Streaking above and below is more
prominent than in other spp. Wings are boldly
barred with pale patch. Has high, sharp "owk-
owk-owk" call and single "keerack" call.
Occurs in mixed woodland in E and N Europe.
Never occurs in British Isles

115

Dark
patches

Barring

Dark

Very long
wings

Pale

Eagle Owl is the largest and most magnificent of all owls and has an enormous wing span. Note large, round head, prominent ears and large orange eyes. Dark breast streaking is usually present. Dark forewing and dark carpal patch contrast with pale primaries. Overall, looks dark and massive in flight. Call is a deep, throaty "woo-hu". Resident over much of Europe, with a wide distribution in afforested and rocky areas. Very rare in British Isles

Circular finely
barred disc

Tiny
eyes

Pale buff
panel

Heavy
barring
(cp Ural)

Great Grey Owl is huge (just smaller than Eagle Owl). Large circular facial disc and tiny round yellow eyes create unmistakable facial appearance. (Face always appears round.) Plumage is mainly grey-black but white markings on back and wings show at rest and in flight. Note pale buff panel showing on wing tips in flight. Cp heavy barring on wing with Ural sp. "Kee-yick" and "hoo-hoo-huh" calls are similar to Tawny but deeper. Occurs in conifer forests of Scandinavia and SE Europe, not in British Isles

Waders

Little Bustard is almost twice Partridge size, and a terrestrial sp of large fields, heaths and waste ground. Heavy body, and black, white and buff plumage distinguish from any other European bird. Fast flight with rapid wingbeats also identifies. (♂'s wings make whistling sound.) Rare vagrant

Black neck

Black

Black

White

Great Bustard is an immense (♂ is much larger than ♀) terrestrial sp with a stately gait. Despite size, merges easily with steppe-like habitat. Shows large areas of white in its slow, ponderous flight (bow-winged like heron). Rare visitor to British Isles

Black border

Pale grey

Very white below (♂, ♀)

Cp Snipe

Cp Snipe

Long-billed Dowitcher (very like Short-billed sp) resembles Snipe in size, bill and appearance, but white back patch and pale edge to wing identify. Annual vagrant to reservoirs and marshes (usually Sept-Nov) but sometimes winters

White (cp Spotted Redshank)

Terek Sandpiper is an active, dashing medium-sized wader. Upperparts are black-flecked greyish and bill is upturned. White on rear wing edge is diagnostic. Bobs like Common sp. "Chita-whit-whit" call. Rare in Britain

Eye stripe

No wing-bar

Pale legs

V

▲ **Pectoral Sandpiper** is a Dunlin-like wader, but larger (smaller than ♀ Ruff). Well-marked upperparts (esp on juv which has stronger "Vs" on back) contrast with streaked breast. Wing-bar is faint. Flight is swift and erratic. Regular vagrant (mainly Aug-Oct) to pools, marshes and reservoirs

White

Cp Pectoral to same scale

Black

Upturned bill

Orange-yellow

117

Dunlin

Dunlin is the typical wader both in shape and in plumage pattern ►

Summer

Winter

Juv autumn

Like other waders, Dunlin has white wing-bar, white patches on either side of tail and back and dark strip on tail and back. Bill shape and call distinguish winter birds. Well-marked juv changes into full winter plumage in Oct

From about Jun-Oct, juv shows well-marked golden upperparts and diagnostic, pale, spotted underparts ▼

Summer adult shows black belly which gradually turns white in autumn, creating patchy appearance initially

Cp bill lengths. Both races occur together. ▼

Southern race

Northern race

Little Stint

Autumn adult moults into grey plumage above with faintly streaked breast and white underparts

◄ Summer adult has rich red upperparts, streaked breast and black belly. Northern race has longer bill, but two greatest extremes are shown (above)

The commonest wader—a small dumpy bird which may be seen on all except the very rockiest shores, as well as on estuaries and mudflats, and by inland pools. May be confused by the inexperienced with a number of wader species, but *fairly long, slightly down-curved bill and high-pitched rasping "sheeeeep" call are diagnostic.* As in other waders, birds are in summer plumage from Apr-Aug and winter plumage from Aug-Mar; birds in different plumages occur together from Aug onwards. Birds normally walk. Flight is swift and twisting with very rapid wingbeats. Swirling flocks show as flickering dark and white masses. Resident, breeding on open moorland throughout British Isles. Also winter visitor and migrant.

Little Stint/Temminck's Stint

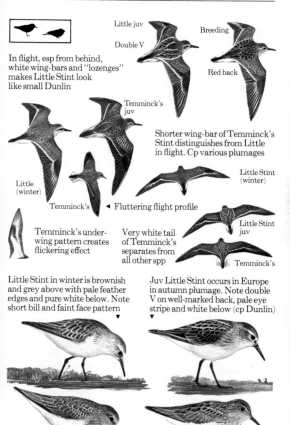

In flight, esp from behind, white wing-bars and "lozenges" makes Little Stint look like small Dunlin

Little juv
Double V
Breeding
Red back

Temminck's juv

Shorter wing-bar of Temminck's Stint distinguishes from Little in flight. Cp various plumages

Little Stint (winter)

Little (winter)

Temminck's ◄ Fluttering flight profile

Temminck's underwing pattern creates flickering effect

Very white tail of Temminck's separates from all other spp

Little Stint juv

Temminck's

Little Stint in winter is brownish and grey above with pale feather edges and pure white below. Note short bill and faint face pattern ▼

Juv Little Stint occurs in Europe in autumn plumage. Note double V on well-marked back, pale eye stripe and white below (cp Dunlin) ▼

Longer profile

Shorter bill

Juv Temminck's is greyish above with double-edged crescent marks. Note darkish breast, very short bill and pale legs

Temminck's Stint is greyish above with black patches in summer but is less strongly marked at end of season (above). (Cp Little sp)

Little Stint is the smallest of the common waders. *Size, bill, legs and less compact profile distinguish species from Dunlin.* Temminck's is roughly the size of Little Stint with wings marginally longer, but looks minute in field. *Pale legs and shorter wing-bar distinguish it from Little Stint* and small size and *amount of white on tail* set it apart from all other waders. Little has flight as Dunlin, but *Temminck's has erratic fluttering flight and may gain height sharply if flushed.* Little has short "dit-dit" call. Temminck's is *a spluttering trill* quite unlike other wader calls. Little is a common passage bird on coast and inland (Apr-May and especially Aug-Oct). Few winter birds. Temminck's has bred in Britain but is an uncommon passage bird.

119

Curlew Sandpiper

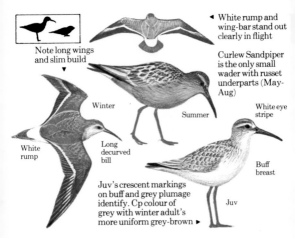

◄ White rump and wing-bar stand out clearly in flight

Note long wings and slim build ▼

Curlew Sandpiper is the only small wader with russet underparts (May-Aug)

Winter

Summer

White eye stripe

White rump

Long decurved bill

Buff breast

Juv's crescent markings on buff and grey plumage identify. Cp colour of grey with winter adult's more uniform grey-brown ►

Juv

Curlew Sandpiper has *longer legs, longer more decurved bill and more elegant proportions than Dunlin*, with which it is often seen. All white underparts of winter birds also distinguish from Dunlin. Feeding, flight and general habits as Dunlin. *Rippling "chirrup" call.* Passage migrant to all coasts in May and Aug-Oct, also often seen inland. Rare in winter.

Broad-billed Sandpiper

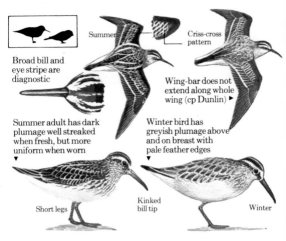

Summer

Criss-cross pattern

Broad bill and eye stripe are diagnostic

Wing-bar does not extend along whole wing (cp Dunlin) ►

Summer adult has dark plumage well streaked when fresh, but more uniform when worn ▼

Winter bird has greyish plumage above and on breast with pale feather edges

Short legs

Kinked bill tip

Winter

Smaller than Dunlin and distinguished from it by the shape of its bill tip (seen in no other wader), *and by unusual face pattern created by the double eye stripes.* Criss-cross pattern on wing panel, and very short legs also separate it from Dunlin and other waders. Deep "chiv-reck" call. Rare but fairly regular visitor May-June and July-Sept.

Purple Sandpiper

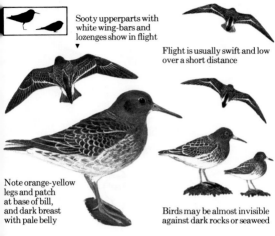

Sooty upperparts with white wing-bars and lozenges show in flight ▼

Flight is usually swift and low over a short distance

Note orange-yellow legs and patch at base of bill, and dark breast with pale belly

Birds may be almost invisible against dark rocks or seaweed

Only sooty-plumaged small wader. Tame birds, restricted to rocky coasts and often found with Turnstone, but winter birds may also occur elsewhere if there are jetties or slipways. White underwing shows when birds hold wings up on landing. *Flight is swift and Dunlin-like.* Usually silent. Mainly winter visitor (Sept-Apr). Passage birds occur inland.

Turnstone

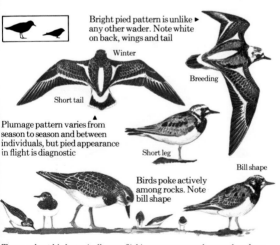

Bright pied pattern is unlike ▶ any other wader. Note white on back, wings and tail

Winter

Breeding

Short tail

Plumage pattern varies from season to season and between individuals, but pied appearance in flight is diagnostic

Short leg

Bill shape

Birds poke actively among rocks. Note bill shape

Tame, robust birds, *typically seen flicking over stones and seaweed* on shore. *Loud, mechanical "tuck-a-tuck" call and rapid series of notes if flushed.* Often occurs with Purple Sandpiper on rocky coasts, but also on shingle and weed-covered flats. Passage migrant (Apr-June, Aug-Oct), sometimes inland. Also winter visitor (some birds stay all summer).

Little Ringed Plover

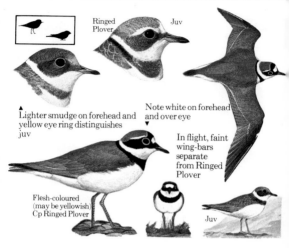

Ringed Plover

Juv

Lighter smudge on forehead and yellow eye ring distinguishes juv

Note white on forehead and over eye ▼

In flight, faint wing-bars separate from Ringed Plover

Flesh-coloured (may be yellowish) Cp Ringed Plover

Juv

Smaller and more delicately built than Ringed Plover, but basically similar in appearance and behaviour. Wings are more obviously flicked in flight, which is more erratic. *Plaintive "pieu" call.* Exclusively inland summer visitor (Apr-Oct) to freshwater areas. Breeds in England but absent from West Country and S coast. Occasional passage bird elsewhere.

Ringed Plover

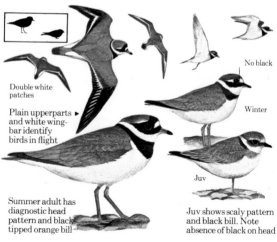

Double white patches

Plain upperparts ▶ and white wing-bar identify birds in flight

No black

Winter

Juv

Summer adult has diagnostic head pattern and black tipped orange bill

Juv shows scaly pattern and black bill. Note absence of black on head

Bullet-shaped head, short bill and contrasting plumage pattern sets apart from other common waders. Often seen running, then pausing to tilt forwards and pick up food. Plumage varies between individuals. Flight swift and erratic with very fast wingbeats. *Lilting "turwilk" call is diagnostic.* Widely distributed throughout British Isles.

Sanderling

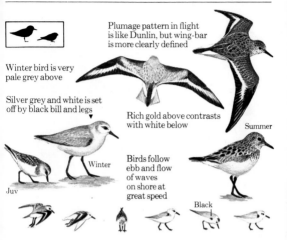

Plumage pattern in flight is like Dunlin, but wing-bar is more clearly defined

Winter bird is very pale grey above

Silver grey and white is set off by black bill and legs

Rich gold above contrasts with white below

Summer

Winter

Birds follow ebb and flow of waves on shore at great speed

Juv

Black

Slightly larger than Dunlin and, in winter, ghostly pale. Identified by white wing-bar (more striking than on any small wader), short, straight black bill and short black legs. Habitually runs at great speed. Typical fast wader flight. Like most waders, glides before landing. *"Twik-twik" call is diagnostic.* Occurs on suitable (esp sandy) shores round British Isles.

Kentish Plover

♂

White collar and face give bird pale look (cp Ringed Plover)

♀

All-black bill distinguishes from Ringed sp

Long legs (cp Ringed Plover)

♂

♀

Juv

Ginger crown and black head pattern are unlike any other plover

More elegant-looking bird than the Ringed Plover with which it is often confused. Compare the body and head shape, longer black legs and bill, less-distinct wing-bar and paler appearance overall. Habits and flight similar to Ringed Plover. *Sharp "whit-whit" call is diagnostic.* Rare summer visitor coast SE England (Apr-Aug). Ceased breeding in Britain.

Golden Plover

Winter bird has gold wash over darkish upperparts with distinct wing-bar on long narrow wings. Note bullet head

Southern

Winter

Summer

Summer

Northern

In Mar-Aug/Sept birds show some black below. The farther south, the less black a bird shows

Cp gold on upperparts of summer and winter birds. Note white armpits on summer bird (cp Grey sp)

◄ Cp 2 extremes of breeding plumage. Cp Grey Plover

Northern   Southern

Feeding birds run, pause and dip suddenly

In winter or on passage, birds gather inland to form arrow, double V or massed flocks

Juv winter

Summer

Winter

Note delicate bill (cp Grey Plover), large eye and pale underparts. Juv is yellower above than adult

Square head held high, deep chest and pointed wings are seen on no other inland plover. Wing stretching often reveals bird's location

Dense flocks of Golden Plover fanning out as they land to feed, are a common feature of certain fields and meadows inland. *At all times, all-white underwing, together with yellow spangling above and dark rump, will easily distinguish from Grey Plover.* On ground runs rapidly (compare "pause-dip" manner of feeding with Lapwing). Flight is very fast on long, narrow rapidly beating wings. *Glides before landing, often holding wings up for a moment after alighting.* Has lovely aerial display with much calling. *Liquid, plaintive "kleeep" whistle is diagnostic*, uttered by single birds or flocks. Bird often stands sentinel on rock. Breeds on upland moor W of line from Humber-Severn and NW and N Ireland.

Grey Plover

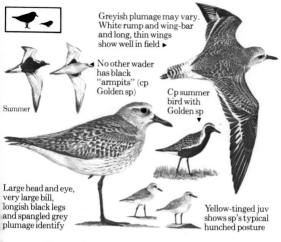

Greyish plumage may vary. White rump and wing-bar and long, thin wings show well in field ▶

No other wader has black "armpits" (cp Golden sp)

Summer

Cp summer bird with Golden sp

Large head and eye, very large bill, longish black legs and spangled grey plumage identify

Yellow-tinged juv shows sp's typical hunched posture

Large, usually wary plover with a bullet head and noticeably stout bill. *Adult in full summer plumage is entirely black and white below.* Fairly fast flight with slower wingbeats than Golden species. *Mournful "clee-er-whee" call is diagnostic.* Winter visitor and passage migrant to coastal flats and estuaries (rare inland) with a few birds seen in summer.

Dotterel

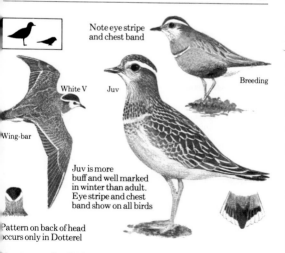

Note eye stripe and chest band

Breeding

White V   Juv

Wing-bar

Juv is more buff and well marked in winter than adult. Eye stripe and chest band show on all birds

Pattern on back of head occurs only in Dotterel

Very tame wader of high mountains in breeding areas, and open country in wintering areas. Never occurs near water. Female is brighter than male. *Head markings and breast band identify winter birds.* Habits and feeding behaviour much as Golden Plover. Call is a low trill. Small breeding population in British mountains. Passage birds, spring and autumn.

Knot

Knot is fat-bodied with long thin wings, fairly short bill, pale rump, white wing-bar and crisp grey plumage

Winter

Winter

White wing-bar and pale rump stand out against dark wings. Note lack of white "lozenge" patches seen in many other waders

Vast, dense flocks of Knot form characteristic patterns—oval if high, and flat-bottomed if low

◀Extreme example of breeding ♂. Many birds may be paler and ♀ is duller

Brown and white feather edges give juv scaly appearance ▼

White eye stripe

Juv

Greenish legs

Summer bird moulting into grey above and white below of winter plumage. Cp summer plumages

Winter

Note stocky build, short straight black bill and greenish legs on all birds

Common medium-sized shore-feeding wader, and much larger than Dunlin with which it is often seen feeding. Often occurs feeding in very large flocks and will be seen walking (never runs) along shore, pausing to probe, often three or four times in one place, for prey. Flight is fast with very rapid wingbeats. *Call is a distinct low "Knot"-like note.* Double "kwik ik" sound may also be heard. Breeds in tundra of Arctic. Some birds occur in summer plumage (birds in British Isles are often deep chesnut colour or head and body), but most are passage migrants and winter visitors, which arrive in vast numbers to frequent mud and sand flats and coastal pools. Occasional birds also occur inland.

Redshank

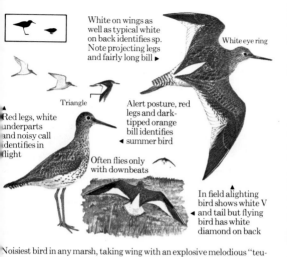

White on wings as well as typical white on back identifies sp. Note projecting legs and fairly long bill ▶

White eye ring

Triangle

Alert posture, red legs and dark-tipped orange bill identifies ◀ summer bird

Red legs, white underparts and noisy call identifies in flight

Often flies only with downbeats

In field alighting bird shows white V ◀ and tail but flying bird has white diamond on back

Noisiest bird in any marsh, taking wing with an explosive melodious "teu-he-he" call. *Only wader with bold white triangle on wing. Legs are red in breeding season and orange in winter.* Flight is erratic with jerky deliberate wingbeats. Very widely distributed throughout British Isles. Breeds on all wet areas inland and coastally. Also passage and winter visitor.

Spotted Redshank

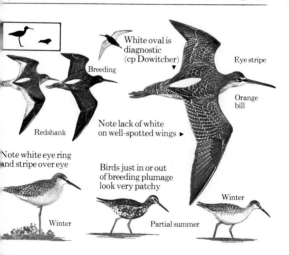

White oval is diagnostic (cp Dowitcher) ▼

Breeding

Eye stripe

Orange bill

Redshank

Note lack of white on well-spotted wings ▶

Note white eye ring and stripe over eye

Birds just in or out of breeding plumage look very patchy

Winter

Winter

Partial summer

Lanky wader, larger than the Redshank with longer bill and legs and lacking white on wings. *White oval and red legs distinguish from all other birds. Breeding birds have sooty black plumage unlike other waders. Loud, deep "cheewit" call is diagnostic.* Passage birds may be seen on coast (May and specially Aug-Oct). Also increasing winter visitor to England.

127

Ruff

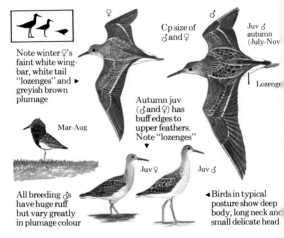

♀   ♂

Cp size of ♂ and ♀

Juv ♂ autumn (July-Nov

Note winter ♀'s faint white wing-bar, white tail "lozenges" and ▶ greyish brown plumage

Mar-Aug

Lozenge

Autumn juv (♂ and ♀) has buff edges to upper feathers. Note "lozenges" ▼

·Juv ♀   Juv ♂

All breeding ♂s have huge ruff but vary greatly in plumage colour

◀ Birds in typical posture show deep body, long neck and small delicate head

Breeding male is unique but most birds seen outside breeding areas in British Isles are juveniles or winter adults. *Pale wing-bar and prominent white patches on all birds identify.* Has flicking action in easy Redshank-like flight. Low "too-wit" call but usually silent. Breeds in a few localities in Britain, also passage migrant and increasing winter visitor.

Common Sandpiper

Flight profile, with bill down, wing slightly ▶ forward and tail partly spread is unique

White outer tail

◀ Note bow-winged profile

White wing-bar

Feeding bird shows clearly ▶ curious shape of white underparts against darker upperparts

◀ Note white eye ring and dark breast with white "slot" against drab olive upperparts

Typical view of flying birds

Extremely active bird with *bobbing head and tail in constant motion.* Easily identified by sober colour and distinctive white wing-bar. When disturbed *flies out in a low arc over water with stiff, flicking wingbeats and uttering "teetering" call.* Summer visitor (Mar-Oct) to be seen by hill streams, lakes and other inland waters. A few winter birds occur.

Wood Sandpiper

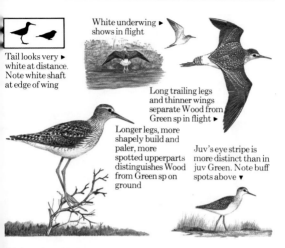

Tail looks very ▶ white at distance. Note white shaft at edge of wing

White underwing ▶ shows in flight

Long trailing legs and thinner wings separate Wood from Green sp in flight ▶

Longer legs, more shapely build and paler, more spotted upperparts distinguishes Wood from Green sp on ground

Juv's eye stripe is more distinct than in juv Green. Note buff spots above ▼

Distinguishing bird on ground may be hard but rump contrasting less starkly with upperparts than in Green, longer projecting legs, *paler underwing and "chip-ip-ip" call identifies on wing*. In flight, usually seen in parties, calling excitedly. Less rapid climb than Green. Passage migrant Apr-May and July-Oct to wet areas inland. Rare breeder in Scotland.

Green Sandpiper

Very dark-looking with ▶ broad wings, white rump and legs only just projecting beyond tail

Eye ring and stripe

On wing, birds ◀ resemble huge House Martins

Note streaked breast and pale head of spring bird

Note black ◀ underwing

Winter

Note dark breast, ◀ well-defined but tiny spots, stocky build and shorter legs than Wood sp

Noisy, easily alarmed bird which *looks almost black and white, with white rump conspicuous in flight*. Typical sandpiper habit of tail and head bobbing. Has twisting, erratic flight with rapid climb after take-off. *Explosive "klerweet-weet" call in flight*. Passage migrant (Apr-June, July-Oct) to wet areas inland and winter visitor (Oct-Apr).

Greenshank

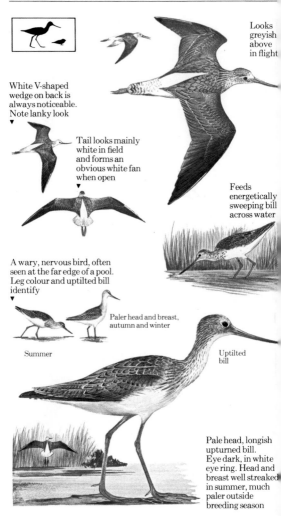

Looks greyish above in flight

White V-shaped wedge on back is always noticeable. Note lanky look ▼

Tail looks mainly white in field and forms an obvious white fan when open ▼

Feeds energetically sweeping bill across water

A wary, nervous bird, often seen at the far edge of a pool. Leg colour and uptilted bill identify ▼

Paler head and breast, autumn and winter

Summer

Uptilted bill

Pale head, longish upturned bill. Eye dark, in white eye ring. Head and breast well streaked in summer, much paler outside breeding season

A lanky, pale wader, larger than Redshank, with plain-coloured, darkish-tipped wings, rather more angular in form than other species. *The only wader with slightly uptilted bill, green legs and white V on back. Back is well marked, and blackish in breeding plumage.* Flight is swift and direct, sometimes high. *Presence is usually indicated by characteristic ringing "tew-tew-tew" call* in emphatic and deliberate manner. Summer visitor to British Isles (late Mar-Oct). On passage is seen frequently on inland waters, sewage farms, coastal pools, creeks and saltings. Breeds in Scotland and Hebrides on moorland. A number of birds winter especially on S and W coasts.

Bar-tailed Godwit

Cp black wing edges ▲ on Black-tailed sp

Summer

Winter

Winter

Cp white V, shorter legs and lack of wing-bar with Black-tailed (also Curlew and Whimbrel)

♀'s bill is longer than ▶ ♂'s

Juv

Juv Black-tailed

Cp juv with juv Black-tailed

Adult feeding

Winter

More stockily built, with a less erect carriage than Black-tailed species. *Summer bird has all-red underparts* (compare with white areas on Black-tailed Godwit). Often seen in loose flocks. Fairly rapid flight. May perform aerobatics on descent. Low chattering call. Winter visitor and passage migrant (often with an influx in May) to coastal flats. Rare inland.

Black-tailed Godwit

Black edges   Summer flock

Note bold wing-bars on flying birds, and "red" summer plumage of displaying birds ▼

Black tail, white rump and wing-bar, and huge bill show well

Winter   Winter

Summer

White

◀ Winter bird is grey-brown and white. Long bill and legs and black tail show on feeding birds

Pair at nest in display ceremony

Long, lanky birds with very long, almost straight bills. Only Oystercatcher has similar white wing-bar. Compare white beneath tail and on belly with Bar-tailed species. Flight is swift, powerful and direct. Has loud "wiker-wiker-wiker" flight call. Resident, breeding in meadowland and marshes in British Isles. Also passage migrant and winter visitor.

Snipe

Very long bill

Display

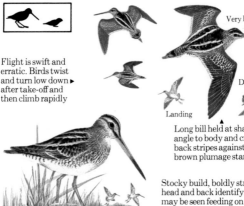

Flight is swift and erratic. Birds twist and turn low down ▶ after take-off and then climb rapidly

Landing

Long bill held at shallow angle to body and creamy back stripes against dark brown plumage stand out

Stocky build, boldly striped head and back identify. Birds may be seen feeding on marshy ground or at water's edge

Medium-sized game bird. Very rarely seen on ground but *dashing zig-zag flight, accompanied by "squelch-like" call,* and brownish, long-billed appearance identifies species once on wing. Has a diving, tail-vibrating display. Resident throughout British Isles. Also winter visitor (Oct-Mar) to any inland wet areas, including fields in winter. Rare on shorelines.

Jack Snipe

Cp profile with snipe. Note broader wings, shorter bill and tail

Back stripes are very vivid on flying bird

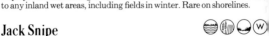

A   B

Cp typical flight paths when flushed: A Snipe; B Jack Snipe

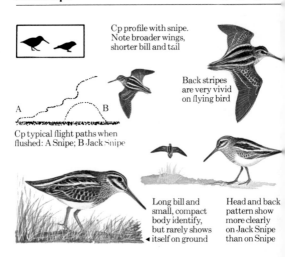

Long bill and small, compact body identify, but rarely shows ◀ itself on ground

Head and back pattern show more clearly on Jack Snipe than on Snipe

Smaller than Snipe and much more secretive, only taking wing at last moment. Usually solitary. Has slower, less zig-zagging flight than Snipe, often flying back over head of intruder or diving into cover after short flight. Usually silent but may give faint Snipe-like call. Winter visitor and passage migrant (Sept-Apr) to marshes and inland waters.

Great Snipe

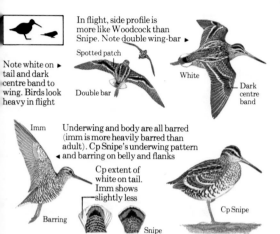

In flight, side profile is more like Woodcock than Snipe. Note double wing-bar ▶

Spotted patch

Note white on ▶ tail and dark centre band to wing. Birds look heavy in flight

Double bar

White

Dark centre band

Imm   Underwing and body are all barred (imm is more heavily barred than adult). Cp Snipe's underwing pattern ◀ and barring on belly and flanks

Cp extent of white on tail. Imm shows slightly less

Barring

Snipe

Cp Snipe

Larger and much more heavily built than Snipe with extremely round body. Considered difficult, but so different from Snipe that it should not be confused. Bill held more horizontal in flight than Snipe. When flushed rises without zig-zagging and drops suddenly to ground after short flight. Usually silent. Annual visitor (Aug-Apr) to British Isles but rarely seen.

Woodcock

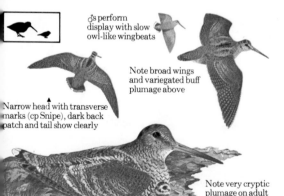

♂s perform display with slow owl-like wingbeats

Note broad wings and variegated buff plumage above

Narrow head with transverse marks (cp Snipe), dark back patch and tail show clearly

Note very cryptic plumage on adult and young, long bill, and large eye set high and far back on head

Clattering take-off, *very fast, twisting flight, profile like a heavy Snipe* and distinctive plumage identify flushed birds. Male displays over a circuit (Mar-July). Has "si-wick" display call but is normally silent. Crepuscular woodland bird, also found on moors in autumn and damper areas such as ditches in winter. Breeds over much of British Isles. Also winter visitor.

Lapwing

White upper tail shows well against dark upperparts ▶

Cp broader wings of ♂ with ♀'s

Flying birds are striking black and white below

♂

♀

Note spiky crest and black breast. Feeding ▶ birds show orange undertail

Note black, white and orange

Crest and black and white plumage identify ▼

Common bird of fields, moors and coastal marshes with an attractive aerial display. *Only species with wispy crest, broad wings and black and white plumage.* Runs or walks on ground, tipping to feed. Usually seen in flocks (may be large). Plaintive "peeerst" or "pee-wit" call. Resident, breeding throughout British Isles. Also winter visitor.

Oystercatcher

Note squat build, long orange ▶ bill, bold wing-bar and black tail with white V up back

White-collared birds are juvs or winter adults

Stabber bill

Hammer bill

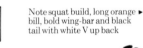

Birds stand waiting for tide to turn, all facing same direction

◀ Birds either hammer molluscs open or stab the muscle which holds shell shut. Method accounts for bill formation

Large, active, noisy birds with piping calls to be seen feeding on muddy or sandy shores, often in huge numbers. *Pied plumage, orange bill and pinkish legs make species unmistakable.* Flies strongly with rather shallow wingbeats. Ringing "kleep-kleep" alarm call and persistent "pic-a-pic" call. Widespread resident, breeding far inland.

Black-winged Stilt

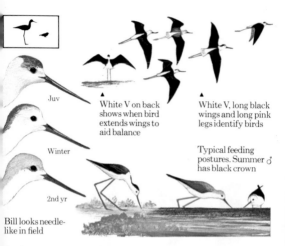

Juv

White V on back
shows when bird
extends wings to
aid balance

White V, long black
wings and long pink
legs identify birds

Winter

Typical feeding
postures. Summer ♂
has black crown

2nd yr

Bill looks needle-
like in field

Combination of legs, bill and plumage are unique. Juvenile has brown crown and second-year bird has grey nape. Male's crown is usually grey-flecked in winter but may be pure white. Breeding female has white crown and nape. Flight is fairly rapid. Rare visitor to shallow fresh or salt water in British Isles (May-Oct). Has nested once (1945).

Avocet

◉ ◉ (S)

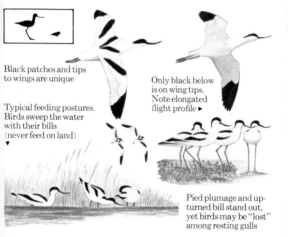

Black patches and tips
to wings are unique

Only black below
is on wing tips.
Note elongated
flight profile ▶

Typical feeding postures.
Birds sweep the water
with their bills
(never feed on land)
▼

Pied plumage and up-
turned bill stand out,
yet birds may be "lost"
among resting gulls

Pied plumage, long, black upturned bill and grey legs make Avocet unmistakable. Young have dark brown where adult has black and slight brownish tinge to upperparts where adult has white. Rapid wingbeats in flight give bird peculiar flickering appearance. Breeds in England (Mar-Oct) mainly in E. Anglia. Rare in winter (mainly on coast in SW England).

Whimbrel

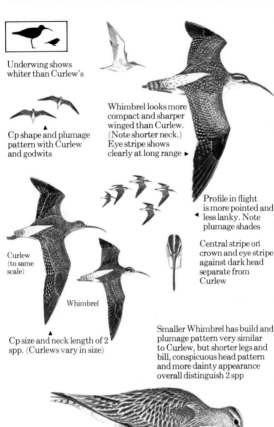

Underwing shows whiter than Curlew's

Cp shape and plumage pattern with Curlew and godwits

Whimbrel looks more compact and sharper winged than Curlew. (Note shorter neck.) Eye stripe shows clearly at long range ►

Profile in flight is more pointed and ◄ less lanky. Note plumage shades

Central stripe on crown and eye stripe against dark head separate from Curlew

Curlew (to same scale)

Whimbrel

Cp size and neck length of 2 spp. (Curlews vary in size)

Smaller Whimbrel has build and plumage pattern very similar to Curlew, but shorter legs and bill, conspicuous head pattern and more dainty appearance overall distinguish 2 spp

Whimbrel has body and wing shape and basic plumage pattern like Curlew, Greenshank and Bar-tailed Godwit. Long down-curved bill sets it apart from all except Curlew, from which it is *best distinguished by head pattern, bill length and quite different call—a series of seven or eight whistles—"qui-hi-hi-hi-hi-hi-hi-hi"* delivered rapidly. Less wary than Curlew but found in the same habitat—muddy or sandy coastal shore and estuaries. Wingbeats are more rapid than Curlew. Call will be heard at night and from high-flying passage birds. Breeds in very limited numbers (200 pairs) on moorland in N of Scotland and Hebrides. Otherwise a passage migrant coastally and inland throughout British Isles.

Curlew

Cp white with Whimbrel, Greenshank and Bar-tailed Godwit

Dark outer wing and patterned ▶ upperparts are almost identical to Whimbrel's but note absence of head pattern on Curlew. Longer bill (esp in ♀) and larger size also identify Curlew, but care is needed

Plain head

Dark outer wing

♀ bill may be up to 15 cm long

♂ bill may be 10-13 cm long

Ringed Plover

Underwing shows as well-marked at close range, but looks white, contrasting with buff chest, at a distance

Flight can be slow and leisurely. Birds may form vast flocks

Resting bird tucks bill into feathers of back and often stands on 1 leg. Cp size with plover

◀ Birds adopt a variety of postures. Whether alert (left) or resting, plumage merges well with grass or moorland

Largest of all waders with a very long, down-curved bill. Can only be confused with Whimbrel. A wary bird, difficult to approach, with a more sedate manner than other waders. Feeds on mud and sand flats and roosts on inland fields, marshes and moorland. Flocks often seen from beach flying low over waves out at sea. Flight is fast but wingbeats are slower than in other waders. Call is diagnostic but very varied, typically a rapid "qui-qui-qui" or a slow "cur-lee". Breeds on moorland, damp pastures, rough land or even in crops over most of British Isles. Also passage migrant, frequently seen inland, and winter visitor (Oct-Mar) to lowlands and coast (where breeding birds also move in winter).

137

Phalaropes

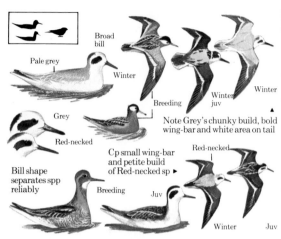

Broad bill

Pale grey

Winter

Breeding

Grey

Red-necked

Winter juv

Winter

Winter

Note Grey's chunky build, bold wing-bar and white area on tail ▲

Bill shape separates spp reliably

Breeding

Cp small wing-bar and petite build of Red-necked sp ▶

Red-necked

Juv

Red-necked

Winter

Juv

Usually seen swimming like miniature gulls. Plumages are complicated. Grey often has yellow at base of bill with pale, greyish or black legs. Red-necked always has black bill and legs. Grey is passage migrant and winter visitor. Red-necked is a summer visitor, breeding in Scottish Isles, also passage migrant (Aug-Oct). Both species are marine in winter.

Stone Curlew

Head and body shape and creeping posture are distinctive. Wing-bar may be dull

Plumage pattern and slow, deep beats of angled wings identify bird in flight

Note large eye, bill, long tail and streaked, sandy plumage

Square-topped head shows from rear ▼

Long pale legs

Variable wing-bar

White patches

Very large, cryptically coloured plover. *Long legs, square head, large staring eye and sandy plumage* are distinctive. Prefers to walk off (mincing gait) rather than to fly. Gives occasional quicker wingbeat in flight. Loud "cour-lee" call, particularly at dusk. Decreasing summer visitor (Mar-Oct/Nov) to England S of line from Wash to Dorset (including Salisbury Plain).

Marsh Birds

Streaked neck

Greenish legs

Bowed wings

Bittern is the only large, buff-coloured, heavily streaked "heron" of the region. Mainly seen at dawn and dusk. Looks vaguely owl-like in flight. "Foghorn" call booms around reed beds. Resident, breeds in England, but is more widespread in winter

Red eye

Streaking

Plumes

Juv

Little Bittern

♂   ♀

Night Heron is a medium-sized heron with unique adult and juv plumage. Note pattern of black and white (and plumes in spring) on adult and heavy spotting on juv. Crepuscular. Rare

♀   ♂

Juv

Green legs

Red on bill

Little Crake is a small, shy marsh bird. Note red on bill and green legs. Cp ♀'s buff underparts with ♀ Baillon's. Occasional visitor (esp spring and autumn)

Little Bittern is a "miniature heron" with dark flight feathers and distinctive pale wing panel. Has "kok-kok" call. Occurs fairly regularly (Apr-Oct)

No red (cp Little)

Tiny spots

Pale legs

Dark crown

Buff

Baillon's Crake is smallest crake. Note well-marked flanks. Cp tiny spots on back with buff streaks of Little. Rare visitor

Spotted Crake is about size of Water Rail, and can be very tame, but easily overlooked. Breeds in Britain, also visitor (esp winter)

Grey Heron

Massive, all-grey bird with trailing legs and black and white head drawn into neck can only be Grey Heron

▲
All-grey pattern of underparts distinguishes Grey from Purple sp

Herons often adopt one-legged stance. Dark-backed juv (left) is rare ▼

Slow, very deep beats of bowed wings identify herons in flight

Imm bird, shown fishing, is distinguished from adult by its head markings (it lacks the black eye stripe) and lack of black on neck and breast ▼

Large size, long legs, mainly grey plumage and long, dagger-like bill identify the Grey Heron. Breeding bird has longer head plumes and white back plumes

Largest common land bird in the British Isles. Size distinguishes from all other birds except the Common Crane, but Crane's extended neck and long, elegant wings distinguish the two species in flight. (Heron may fly with neck extended for short distances.) Favours fresh water for feeding, hunting stealthily by day or night in shallows for fish, amphibians, and the occasional small mammal or water bird. Now preys on fish in urban ponds. May be seen alone or in groups in fields. *Call very harsh "hraak"*, often heard from flying birds. Colonial nester in trees. Occurs throughout the British Isles, frequenting any water where there are fish, particularly marshland but also upland and urban areas.

Purple Heron

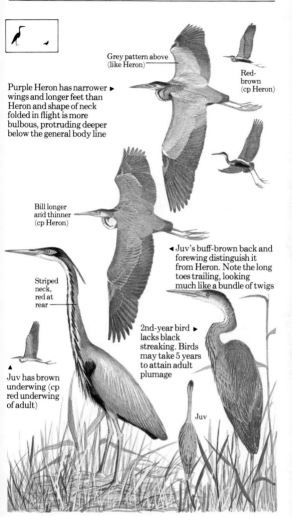

Grey pattern above
(like Heron)

Red-
brown
(cp Heron)

► Purple Heron has narrower
wings and longer feet than
Heron and shape of neck
folded in flight is more
bulbous, protruding deeper
below the general body line

Bill longer
and thinner
(cp Heron)

◄ Juv's buff-brown back and
forewing distinguish it
from Heron. Note the long
toes trailing, looking
much like a bundle of twigs

Striped
neck,
red at
rear

2nd-year bird ►
lacks black
streaking. Birds
may take 5 years
to attain adult
plumage

▲
Juv has brown
underwing (cp
red underwing
of adult)

Juv

Has appearance of scaled-down version of a larger bird, so can look
deceptively large in flight, but any flying view will show the *diagnostic
profile of the folded neck and trailing feet. Habits much like Heron; flight has
the same deep, slow beats of the bowed wings but is more buoyant.* Creeps in
deliberate "slow-motion" manner when hunting in shallows—typical
Heron behaviour. Needs large areas of reed bed for its nesting. Occurs
mostly in S Europe, but birds are distributed widely (Holland has about
900 nesting pairs). Winters in Africa flying high on passage. Some birds
visit England, occurring particularly on E coast (May-Oct), and are
increasingly common. A few have summered.

Rare and Occasional Marsh Birds

Little Egret is a medium-sized white "heron", slim and elegant with 2 long head plumes and fluffy back plumes in breeding season. Note long, thin black bill, black legs and bright yellow feet, which show well in flight. Usually seen in or near water (fresh or saline) and often dashes through shallows after prey. Occurs mainly in S Europe but an increasing visitor to Britain, esp Apr-June, but may occur at any time

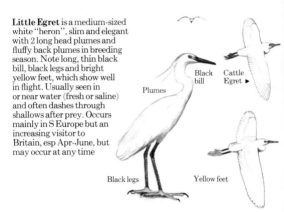

Black bill

Cattle Egret ▶

Plumes

Black legs

Yellow feet

Winter

Buff plumes

Breeding

Cattle Egret is smaller and stouter than Little sp with buff head, breast and back plumes in breeding season. Adults out of breeding season, and juvs are all white. Breeding birds have reddish or yellowish bill and reddish feet (greenish and yellow rest of year). Almost always found feeding near cattle, also on rubbish dumps. Spreading in Europe, rare in British Isles

Spoonbill is a fairly large bird, heron-like in general shape but distinguished by bill shape, and, in flight, by extended neck and flat wings. Has buff breast band and crest in breeding season. Juv has black wing tips. Visitor to British Isles (May-Oct)

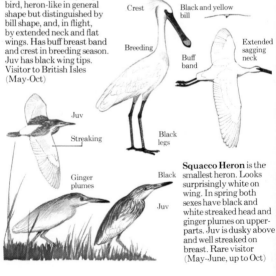

Crest

Black and yellow bill

Breeding

Extended sagging neck

Buff band

Black legs

Juv

Streaking

Ginger plumes

Black

Juv

Squacco Heron is the smallest heron. Looks surprisingly white on wing. In spring both sexes have black and white streaked head and ginger plumes on upper-parts. Juv is dusky above and well streaked on breast. Rare visitor (May-June, up to Oct)

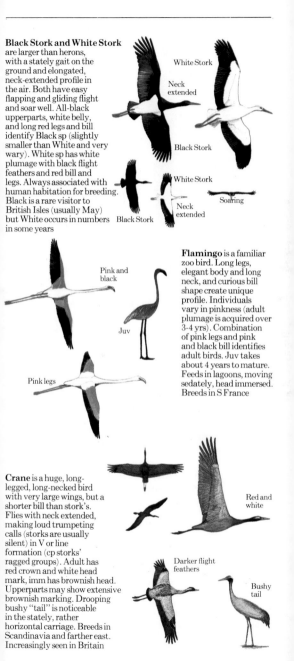

Black Stork and White Stork
are larger than herons,
with a stately gait on the
ground and elongated,
neck-extended profile in
the air. Both have easy
flapping and gliding flight
and soar well. All-black
upperparts, white belly,
and long red legs and bill
identify Black sp (slightly
smaller than White and very
wary). White sp has white
plumage with black flight
feathers and red bill and
legs. Always associated with
human habitation for breeding.
Black is a rare visitor to
British Isles (usually May)
but White occurs in numbers
in some years

White Stork

Neck
extended

Black Stork

White Stork

Neck
extended

Soaring

Black Stork

Pink and
black

Juv

Pink legs

Flamingo is a familiar
zoo bird. Long legs,
elegant body and long
neck, and curious bill
shape create unique
profile. Individuals
vary in pinkness (adult
plumage is acquired over
3-4 yrs). Combination
of pink legs and pink
and black bill identifies
adult birds. Juv takes
about 4 years to mature.
Feeds in lagoons, moving
sedately, head immersed.
Breeds in S France

Crane is a huge, long-
legged, long-necked bird
with very large wings, but a
shorter bill than stork's.
Flies with neck extended,
making loud trumpeting
calls (storks are usually
silent) in V or line
formation (cp storks'
ragged groups). Adult has
red crown and white head
mark, imm has brownish head.
Upperparts may show extensive
brownish marking. Drooping
bushy "tail" is noticeable
in the stately, rather
horizontal carriage. Breeds in
Scandinavia and farther east.
Increasingly seen in Britain

Red and
white

Darker flight
feathers

Bushy
tail

143

Divers

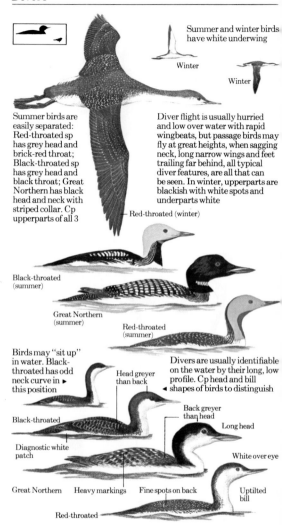

Summer and winter birds have white underwing

Winter

Winter

Summer birds are easily separated: Red-throated sp has grey head and brick-red throat; Black-throated sp has grey head and black throat; Great Northern has black head and neck with striped collar. Cp upperparts of all 3

Diver flight is usually hurried and low over water with rapid wingbeats, but passage birds may fly at great heights, when sagging neck, long narrow wings and feet trailing far behind, all typical diver features, are all that can be seen. In winter, upperparts are blackish with white spots and underparts white

Red-throated (winter)

Black-throated (summer)

Great Northern (summer)

Red-throated (summer)

Birds may "sit up" in water. Black-throated has odd neck curve in ► this position

Head greyer than back

Divers are usually identifiable on the water by their long, low profile. Cp head and bill ◄ shapes of birds to distinguish

Black-throated

Back greyer than head

Long head

Diagnostic white patch

White over eye

Great Northern   Heavy markings   Fine spots on back   Uptilted bill

Red-throated

The Red-throated is the smallest and most common of the three diver species occurring in the British Isles. All are superficially Cormorant-like but distinguished by a thicker tube-like neck and pointed bill. Legs are set well back and birds are virtually tailless. Long narrow wings set mid-way along the body give the body a characteristic flight profile. Keeling over in water to reveal underside and just touching water with tip of bill are typical diver habits. May also put head underwater briefly before diving, often for long distances. Red-throated Diver will jump dive or slip under. Winters (Aug-Apr) sometimes in numbers, usually singly or in loose groups. May well occur inland. Breeds N Ireland and along W coast of Scotland.

Black-throated sp is larger than Red-throated (but hard to tell in flight). Has darkest back of 3 spp and very grey head and neck. Juv is more heavily ◄ marked on its back than adult

Black-throated

Red-throated sp

Black-throated sp has most regular bill of 3

Great Northern sp has heavy angular bill

Great Northern Diver is much the largest of the 3 spp. It has very long wings which flex noticeably at the tip. Pronounced forehead and heavy, deep bill create head profile much less fine than in other 2 spp. Angular, rather lumpy body is distinctively marked with a more or less regular pattern of barring which may vary ◄ between individual birds

Great Northern (winter)

Winter   Summer

Black-throated

Winter   Summer

Great Northern

Typical views of Great Northern sp on water

Breeding plumage

Red-throated   Black-throated

Great Northern Diver is a winter visitor to coastal waters (Sept–May), although, as with all divers, individual birds may occur inland spending much of winter on a reservoir. Birds wintering at sea are highly susceptible to damage by oil. Some Great Northern Divers may remain for the summer months, frequenting islands in the north of Britain. Has bred, but very rarely, in Scotland, and may yet establish itself as a regular breeding species. Black-throated Diver is the least common of the three species, wintering on the coast, with occasional birds occurring inland. Breeds on W coast of Scotland, the Hebrides and on islets in lochs, but is vulnerable to disturbance, which affects breeding success.

Black-necked Grebe

Cp size with Little Grebe below ▼

Extent of white wing panel

Note sharp contrast of black and white on head

Note head shape, bill and white on face

High forehead

Turned up bill tip

Golden fan

Summer

Profile can be deceptive. Both spp may sit high or low in water with neck extended or tucked into back

Slightly smaller than Slavonian Grebe, and distinguished by different shape of forehead, uptilted bill and area of black on head. Often seen in company with other grebes. Dives well, but feeds more from surface than other species. Fairly common on inland water and sheltered marine areas of British Isles (Aug-Mar). Scattered breeding in England, Scotland and Ireland.

Slavonian Grebe

⬲ ⛰ Ⓡ

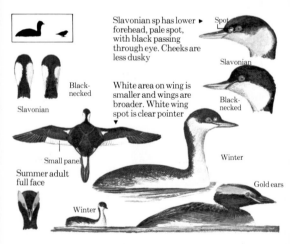

Slavonian sp has lower ▶ forehead, pale spot, with black passing through eye. Cheeks are less dusky

Spot

Slavonian

Black-necked

Slavonian

White area on wing is smaller and wings are broader. White wing spot is clear pointer ▼

Black-necked

Small panel

Winter

Summer adult full face

Winter

Gold ears

Habits generally identical to Black-necked Grebe, but takes flight rather more frequently, though both will often swim off rather than fly. Usually jumps to dive (Black-necked goes straight under). Winters on inland waters but more marine than Black-necked and more at home in rougher water. Breeds in restricted numbers in a few places in Scotland.

Great Crested Grebe

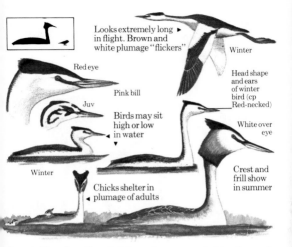

Looks extremely long in flight. Brown and white plumage "flickers"

Winter

Red eye

Pink bill

Juv

Head shape and ears of winter bird (cp Red-necked)

White over eye

Birds may sit high or low in water

Winter

Chicks shelter in plumage of adults

Crest and frill show in summer

Largest of the grebes with marked changes in summer and winter plumage. A long, thin-looking bird, especially in winter when its very thin white neck with narrow, black stripe at the rear stands out. Expert diver, and swims off or dives rather than flies. Growling call. Occurs in suitable British Isles waters except in far N Scotland, moving to larger expanses, Oct-Mar.

Red-necked Grebe

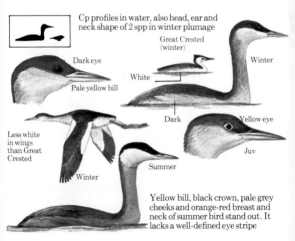

Cp profiles in water, also head, ear and neck shape of 2 spp in winter plumage

Great Crested (winter)

Dark eye

White

Pale yellow bill

Winter

Dark

Yellow eye

Less white in wings than Great Crested

Winter

Summer

Juv

Yellow bill, black crown, pale grey cheeks and orange-red breast and neck of summer bird stand out. It lacks a well-defined eye stripe

Smaller than the Great Crested species and easily identifiable in summer. *Head and body shape, yellow on bill and lack of white above eye distinguish the Red-necked in winter.* Expert diver, like all grebes. Normally a winter visitor (Aug-Apr), found inland or at sea, but has summered. Usually seen singly. Greatest numbers Oct-Mar.

Water Rail

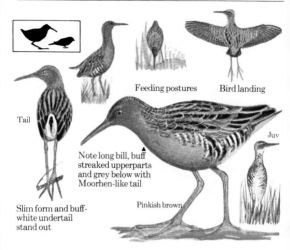

Feeding postures

Bird landing

Tail

Note long bill, buff streaked upperparts and grey below with Moorhen-like tail

Juv

Slim form and buff-white undertail stand out

Pinkish brown

Loud, pig-like squealing and staccato "kik-ik-ik" calls are often only indication of its presence, but bird will emerge from cover if all is quiet. May be seen clambering in bushes. Has weak, leg-trailing flight, very like Moorhen. Breeds in limited numbers throughout British Isles, in reed beds, marshes and swampy rivers, but occurs more widely in winter.

Little Grebe

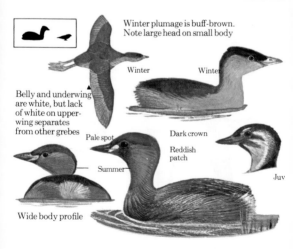

Winter plumage is buff-brown. Note large head on small body

Winter

Winter

Belly and underwing are white, but lack of white on upper-wing separates from other grebes

Pale spot

Dark crown

Reddish patch

Summer

Juv

Wide body profile

Smallest of the grebes, showing a high, round-bodied profile in the water and fluffy, square-ended rear. Unlike other grebes, has no white in wings. Energetic diver, disappearing with a great flourish. Often patters along surface to keep its distance. Flight is fast with rapid wingbeats. Found in quite small areas of fresh water, visiting larger expanses in winter.

Coot

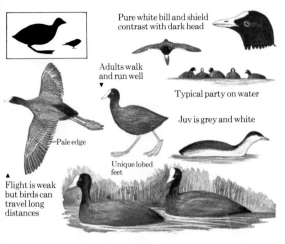

Pure white bill and shield contrast with dark head

Adults walk and run well

Typical party on water

Juv is grey and white

Pale edge

Unique lobed feet

Flight is weak but birds can travel long distances

Noisy, quarrelsome bird, common on inland waters (including park lakes), and *instantly recognizable by its white bill and frontal plate.* Body is round and blue-grey, but black-looking from a distance. Birds often graze in groups near water. Loud explosive "keuk", "k-towk" and "t'uck" calls. Resident. Moves from higher exposed waters in winter.

Moorhen

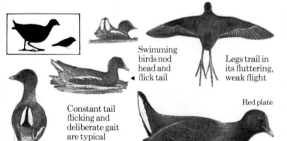

Swimming birds nod head and flick tail

Legs trail in its fluttering, weak flight

Constant tail flicking and deliberate gait are typical

Red plate

Red and yellow bill

Juv is two-tone buff-brown with green frontal plate

Greenish yellow legs

Very common bird of park lakes, rivers, streams and ponds throughout British Isles, and tame where not molested. *Red frontal plate and bill with yellow tip,* dark-looking plumage with *white flank line and undertail* are unmistakable. Runs, walks, swims and dives with ease. Explosive "kurruk" and "kityik" calls and softer "kok-kok" call at night.

Wigeon

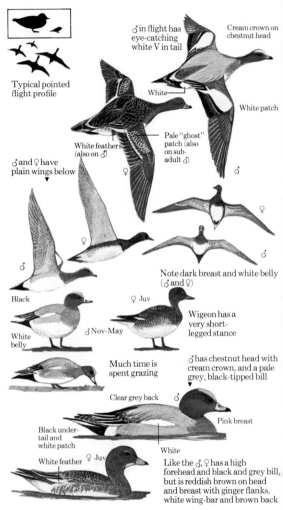

Typical pointed flight profile

♂ in flight has eye-catching white V in tail

Cream crown on chestnut head

White

White patch

Pale "ghost" patch (also on sub-adult ♂)

White feathers (also on ♂)

♀

♂

♂ and ♀ have plain wings below

♀

♀

♂

Note dark breast and white belly (♂ and ♀)

Black

White belly

♂ Nov-May

♀ Juv

Wigeon has a very short-legged stance

Much time is spent grazing

♂ has chestnut head with cream crown, and a pale grey, black-tipped bill

Clear grey back

♂

Black under-tail and white patch

Pink breast

White feather ♀ Juv

White

Like the ♂, ♀ has a high forehead and black and grey bill, but is reddish brown on head and breast with ginger flanks, white wing-bar and brown back

Delicately featured ducks with noticeably sharp silhouette and fairly short necks. Surface-feeding duck that dives only if injured, and does not normally up-end. Spends more time feeding on land than any other duck, and may be seen grazing on short or marine grass in large numbers. Fast, direct flight typical of most ducks, and, like other surface-feeding ducks, leaps from water straight into flight. Male has a far-carrying penetrating "whee-oooo" call. Extremely gregarious, occurring in large numbers either inland or on coast. Large continental influx to British Isles in winter. Breeds in scattered localities in Scotland and, less commonly, in England. Often seen on coast in association with Brent Geese.

Pintail

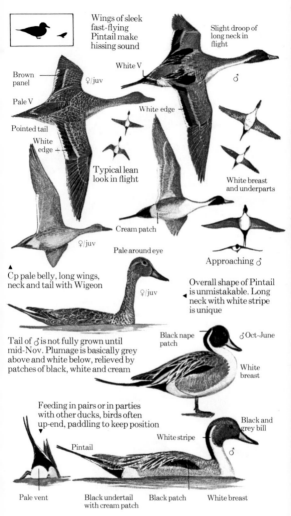

Wings of sleek fast-flying Pintail make hissing sound

Slight droop of long neck in flight

♂

White V

Brown panel

♀/juv

Pale V

White edge

Pointed tail

White edge

Typical lean look in flight

White breast and underparts

♀/juv

Cream patch

Pale around eye

Approaching ♂

♀/juv

▲ Cp pale belly, long wings, neck and tail with Wigeon

Overall shape of Pintail is unmistakable. Long neck with white stripe is unique ◄

Tail of ♂ is not fully grown until mid-Nov. Plumage is basically grey above and white below, relieved by patches of black, white and cream

Black nape patch

♂ Oct.-June

White breast

Feeding in pairs or in parties with other ducks, birds often up-end, paddling to keep position

Pintail

Black and grey bill

White stripe

♂

Pale vent

Black undertail with cream patch

Black patch

White breast

More shy and wary than other ducks, keeping its distance and quick to take flight. *The long-tailed, boldly patterned male is unmistakable* with an elegant attenuated profile in flight. *Female is identifiable by bill colour and plumage pattern*, and is paler and greyer with less warm colours than female Mallard or Gadwall. Feeds in shallow water, up-ending for worms and other aquatic invertebrates. Flight is usually high and very fast with rapid wingbeats, though it may be more leisurely as birds circle before landing. Occurs mainly in winter (Oct–Apr), especially in flood waters and sheltered estuarine areas. Breeds only rarely in scattered localities throughout British Isles.

Gadwall

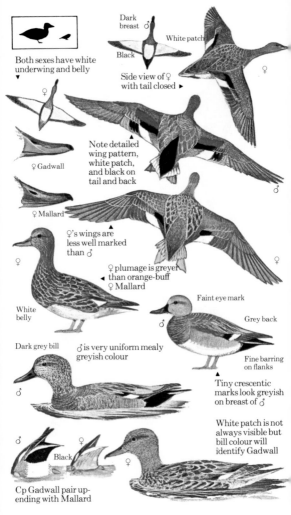

Both sexes have white underwing and belly ▼

Dark breast ♂

White patch

Black

Side view of ♀ with tail closed ►

♀ Gadwall

♀ Mallard

Note detailed wing pattern, white patch, and black on tail and back ▲

♀'s wings are less well marked than ♂ ▲

♀ plumage is greyer than orange-buff ♀ Mallard ◄

White belly

Dark grey bill

♂ is very uniform mealy greyish colour

Faint eye mark

Grey back

Fine barring on flanks

Tiny crescentic marks look greyish on breast of ♂ ▲

White patch is not always visible but bill colour will identify Gadwall

Black

Cp Gadwall pair up-ending with Mallard

Rather inconspicuous and soberly marked ducks, but *easily identifiable by the white patch in the wing* and (less easy to see) its rather more pointed wings and less heavy profile than Mallard. Shyer and more retiring than Mallard and essentially a bird of freshwater, rarely seen on the sea. Up-ends to feed. Flight similar but less ponderous than Mallard, with faster wingbeats. Male's call is series of whistles and grunts. Female has progressively softer quacking call somewhat like female Mallard. Breeds in scattered localities throughout British Isles but especially in E Anglia. Otherwise winter visitor (Oct-Mar) in limited numbers. Spreading locally (usually after introduction to local ponds).

Mallard

Long, neck and purple band on fast-beating wings, set far back, show well in its rapid flight

White neck ring

Black wedge

Purple

Grey shade (unlike any other duck)

Double white wing-bars

♀

♂

♀

♂ and ♀ have white forewing below

Green head, white neck and dark upper breast contrast sharply in ♂. Note all-yellow bill and curled feathers in tail (only on ♂)

♀ and juv have streaked body and white wing linings unlike any other duck except ♀ Shoveler, but bill shape sets spp apart. Note juv's yellow feet

Yellow bill

Only on ♂ Mallard

Orange legs

Cp Gadwall

Juv

Yellowish

Note black central wedge with pale area either side

Birds up-ending

Bill colour separates ♀ and imm from Gadwall

♀

♂

◀ Dark line on flank with grey shades below and above is peculiar to ♂

Most widespread duck in the British Isles and a common sight in town parks and village ponds. A fairly heavy bird in weight and proportion, but a good flier which also walks well. Feeds by up-ending and dabbling, but birds may be seen well away from water in spring and will graze in fields after harvest and in winter. Swims high in water. Young birds dive well, but adults dive only when injured. Male has soft call and female the familiar deep "quack-quack" repeated more and more softly. Mallard is both a freshwater and marine species and may be seen resting on the open sea. Breeds on both large and small areas of water, and may occasionally nest in tree holes. Also winter visitor (Sept-Apr).

153

Teal

Green and black stripes

♀   ♂

Pale belly of ♂ and ♀ show in flight. ♂ has cream breast

Tiny size and black bill and legs identify ♀

Note ♂'s red and green head, striking white wing-bar and white V above tail ▶

♂

♀

♀'s bar and panels show well in flight ▼

Stripes

♀   ♀   ♂

Cream and black panels

Smallest of the ducks (smaller than a pigeon), and size alone will usually identify, but *wing pattern distinguishes birds from the similar-sized Garganey* (Mar-Sept only). Surface feeder. Very swift, wheeling, wader-like flight with rapid wingbeats. Male has short, ringing "kwit-kwit" call. Resident and winter visitor distributed throughout the British Isles.

Garganey

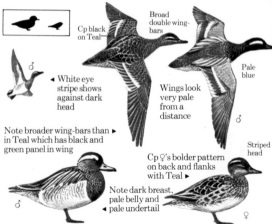

Cp black on Teal

Broad double wing-bars

♂

◀ White eye stripe shows against dark head

Note broader wing-bars than ▶ in Teal which has black and green panel in wing

Wings look very pale from a distance

Pale blue

♂

Striped head

Cp ♀'s bolder pattern on back and flanks with Teal ▶

♂

Note dark breast, pale belly and ◀ pale undertail

♀

Tiny duck, only confusable with similar-sized Teal. Head and wing pattern, sharply demarcated breast and curved grey scapulars make male easy to identify. Pattern on female's wings looks dull brown and grey. *Crackling, football-rattle-like call is diagnostic.* Rare breeder in British Isles. Also summer visitor (early Mar-Sept/Oct) to freshwater marshes and rivers.

Shoveler

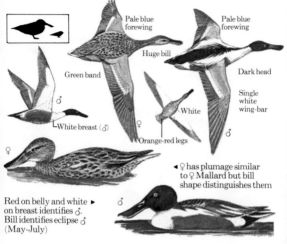

Pale blue forewing

Pale blue forewing

Huge bill

Green band

Dark head

Single white wing-bar

♂

└White breast (♂)

White

♀

Orange-red legs

♂

◄ ♀ has plumage similar to ♀ Mallard but bill shape distinguishes them

Red on belly and white ► on breast identifies ♂. Bill identifies eclipse ♂ (May-July)

♂

Huge, spatulate bill easily distinguishes Shoveler from other ducks. *Wings appear set far back in flight due to long neck and bill.* Rises easily and flies with rapid wingbeats. Sits low in front on water, dabbling with bill. Inhabits freshwater lakes, marshes, ponds and sewage farms. Breeds in scattered localities throughout UK. Also winter visitor (Sept-Apr).

Ferruginous Duck

 RV

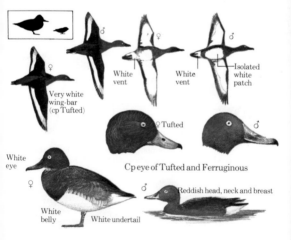

♂

♀

♂

♀

White vent

White vent

Isolated white patch

Very white wing-bar (cp Tufted)

♀ Tufted

♂

White eye

Cp eye of Tufted and Ferruginous

♀

♂

Reddish head, neck and breast

White belly

White undertail

Slimmer, more Teal-shaped and shyer than the squat Tufted Duck. *White eye, belly and undertail* are distinctive. *Male's deep reddish plumage is unlike any other duck.* Female has rufous chocolate plumage and white wing-bar. Up-ends and dives but also feeds on surface. Flight and take-off is easier than in Tufted Duck. A few winter visitors (especially SE England).

155

Pochard

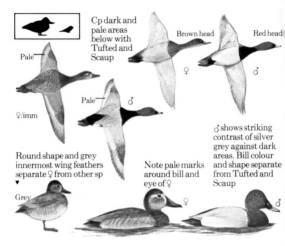

Cp dark and pale areas below with Tufted and Scaup

Pale

Brown head

Red head

♀

♂

♀/imm

Pale

♂

Round shape and grey innermost wing feathers separate ♀ from other sp ▼

Grey

Note pale marks around bill and eye of ♀

♀

♂ shows striking contrast of silver grey against dark areas. Bill colour and shape separate from Tufted and Scaup

♂

Squat, round-looking ducks, expert at diving and rarely seen on land. Head and bill shape will usually identify. Often occurs in large flocks. Birds patter across surface to take off. Wingbeats are rapid in flight. Occurs on fresh water also occasionally at sea. Breeds throughout most of British Isles. Also winter visitor.

Red-crested Pochard

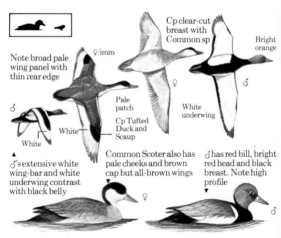

Cp clear-cut breast with Common sp

Bright orange

♀/imm

Note broad pale wing panel with thin rear edge

♂

Pale patch

Cp Tufted Duck and Scaup

White

White

♀

White underwing

♂

♂'s extensive white wing-bar and white underwing contrast with black belly

Common Scoter also has pale cheeks and brown cap but all-brown wings

♀

♂ has red bill, bright red head and black breast. Note high profile

♂

Portly, large-headed diving duck. Sits rather high in water and has longer profile than Pochard. *Male is only freshwater duck with black belly*, which shows clearly against white flanks and wings. Occurs only on fresh water. Scattered breeder in S England, also few annual wild visitors, especially to E Anglia.

Long-tailed Duck

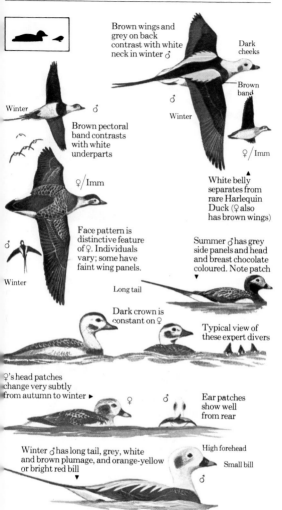

Brown wings and grey on back contrast with white neck in winter ♂

Dark cheeks

Brown band

♂

Winter

Winter ♂

Brown pectoral band contrasts with white underparts

♀/Imm

White belly separates from rare Harlequin Duck (♀ also has brown wings)

♀/Imm

Face pattern is distinctive feature of ♀. Individuals vary; some have faint wing panels.

♂

Winter

Summer ♂ has grey side panels and head and breast chocolate coloured. Note patch

Long tail

Dark crown is constant on ♀

Typical view of these expert divers

♀'s head patches change very subtly from autumn to winter ▶

♀ ♂

Ear patches show well from rear

Winter ♂ has long tail, grey, white and brown plumage, and orange-yellow or bright red bill ▼

High forehead

Small bill

♂

Beautiful Long-tailed male is unmistakable in any plumage. *Female is a fairly small bird distinguished by the combination of its head and bill shape with a smudgy dark and pale pattern.* Long-tailed Ducks are essentially marine birds, often seen well out at sea, though they occur singly on coastal pools or inland reservoirs. Expert divers quite at home in rough seas, they usually show characteristic low head profile on water. Very energetic birds in flight with deep wingbeats below body, unlike any other duck. Flight parties may be seen carrying out peculiar rolling action. Very local bird with a variety of yodelling, hound-like calls. Common winter visitor in N Scotland and a regular visitor to SE England, especially Oct–Mar.

157

Tufted Duck

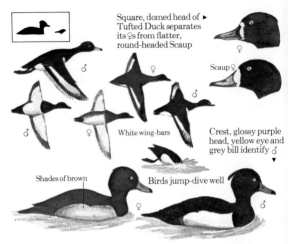

Square, domed head of ▶
Tufted Duck separates
its ♀s from flatter,
round-headed Scaup

Scaup ♀

♂

♀

♀

♂

White wing-bars

Crest, glossy purple
head, yellow eye and
grey bill identify ♂
▼

Shades of brown

Birds jump-dive well

♀

♂

Small, round, very active ducks, *continually jump-diving and bobbing up to surface*. Male is unmistakable but female and young need care to tell apart from larger, longer-bodied Scaup. White undertail of some females may cause confusion with Ferruginous Duck. Flight is rapid with pattering take-off. Common resident and winter visitor (Oct-Apr).

Scaup

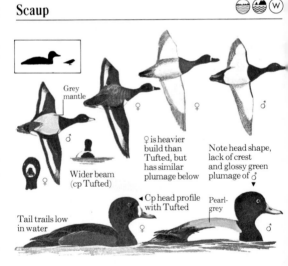

Grey
mantle

♂

♀

♀

♂

♀

Wider beam
(cp Tufted)

♀ is heavier
build than
Tufted, but
has similar
plumage below

Note head shape,
lack of crest
and glossy green
plumage of ♂

◀ Cp head profile
with Tufted

Pearl-
grey

Tail trails low
in water

♀

♂

Larger than the closely related Tufted Duck with a longer, wider body. A marine species also found on pools close to the coast but uncommon far inland. Occurs in numbers near mussel-beds and sewage outfalls. Regular winter visitor (mid-Sept-Apr/May). Breeds very rarely in Scotland. Males less common in S, where females and juveniles are usually seen.

Smew

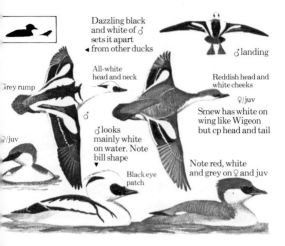

Dazzling black and white of ♂ sets it apart from other ducks ◄

♂ landing

Grey rump

All-white head and neck

Reddish head and white cheeks

♀/juv

Smew has white on wing like Wigeon but cp head and tail

♀/juv

♂ looks mainly white on water. Note bill shape ▼

Black eye patch

Note red, white and grey on ♀ and juv

Smallest and shortest billed of the sawbills. Black and white of male and plumage combination of female and juvenile distinguish from other ducks. Sits high in water and dives expertly, sometimes in pairs or small groups. Flies in oblique, waving lines or in loose groups. Winter visitor (Nov-Apr), usually occurs in fresh water in SE England.

Goldeneye

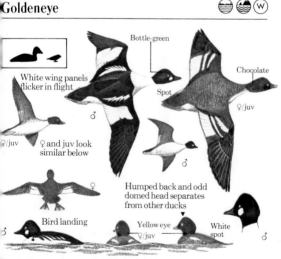

Bottle-green

White wing panels flicker in flight

Chocolate

Spot

♀/juv

♂

♀/juv

♀ and juv look similar below

♂

Humped back and odd domed head separates from other ducks

Bird landing

♂

Yellow eye

♀/juv

White spot

♂

Small, dumpy, short-necked birds. Goldeneye are expert under water, jumping to dive and staying under for long periods. *Flight is very swift (male's wings whistle).* Birds patter along surface to take off, drakes flickering black and white. Mainly winter visitor (Oct-Mar/Apr) to shallow estuaries, bays or lakes. Few breed in NW England and N Scotland.

Goosander

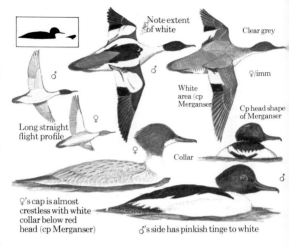

Note extent of white

Clear grey

♂

♂

♀/imm

White area (cp Merganser)

Long straight flight profile

♀

Cp head shape of Merganser

Collar

♂

♀'s cap is almost crestless with white collar below red head (cp Merganser)

♂'s side has pinkish tinge to white

Largest sawbilled duck with rather broad wings and a heavy, rectangular body. *Pinkish tinge of male stands out from a distance.* Dives well and for some distance. Usually silent. Red-headed females and juveniles arrive before males. Breeds by rivers and lakes in England N of Lancashire and (rarely) in Wales and Ireland. Also a winter visitor (Oct-Mar).

Red-breasted Merganser

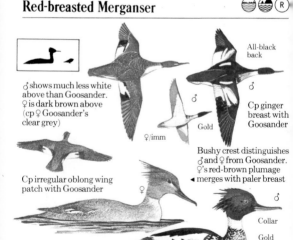

All-black back

♂ shows much less white above than Goosander. ♀ is dark brown above (cp ♀ Goosander's clear grey)

♂

♂

Gold

♀/imm

Cp ginger breast with Goosander

Bushy crest distinguishes ♂ and ♀ from Goosander. ♀'s red-brown plumage ◄ merges with paler breast

Cp irregular oblong wing patch with Goosander

♀

♂

Collar

Gold

Long red bill, long body and crest distinguish Merganser from other ducks. *Distinctly smaller and more delicately proportioned than Goosander* (a clear distinction in flight). Usually silent. Much more marine than Goosander. Ground nester by rivers and lakes in W Britain, from S Wales to Shetland. Also winter visitor (Oct-Mar), uncommon inland except Ireland.

Shelduck

Red knob

Breeding ♂

Black belly

Goose-like shape and pied plumage identifies ♂ and ♀

♀ has almost no black on belly

Adult pairs may have a flotilla of chicks from several broods

Juv is duller but is identified by shape of head and body

Rear view of pied plumage

Birds feed by dabbling or up-ending

No breast band

Neither duck nor goose; *distinguishable from ducks by its larger size and colourful, pied appearance.* Sociable bird, usually seen feeding on mud or sand flats, pools or shorelines. More rapid wingbeats than geese, but flight is slower. Wings held well forward on take-off. Male call is a series of high whistles. Resident round British Isles coasts, also nests inland.

Eider

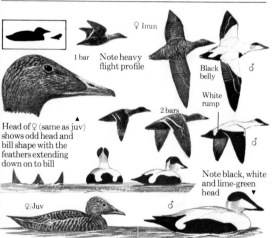

♀ Imm

1 bar   Note heavy flight profile

Black belly

White rump

♂

2 bars

♂

Head of ♀ (same as juv) shows odd head and bill shape with the feathers extending down on to bill

Note black, white and lime-green head

♀/Juv   ♂

Large size, peculiar head shape and male's pied plumage distinguish Eider from all other ducks. Immature birds have patchy plumage. Exclusively marine, seen on open shore and islands, and highly gregarious. Expert diver and swimmer. Flight is slow and take-off laboured. Soft "coo-ooh" call. Breeds round coast of Scotland, N England and N Ireland.

Feral and Rare Water Birds

King Eider is slightly smaller than Eider. ♀ is very like Eider but has smaller feather lobe on bill. ♂'s black and white plumage is unmistakable in flight. Arctic sp rare

♀

♂

Steep forehead

Unique face pattern

Cp white on Eider

White panels

Steller's Eider is small with white patchy ▶ head. ♂'s orange underparts are unique in marine duck. Mallard-like wing pattern of ♀ is also unusual. Arctic sp rare visitor to N Britain

♀

♂

Green and black

Eye ring

Cp Mallard

Black spot

Cp ♂ Smew (at distance)

♀

White patch

♂

Cocked tail

Blue bill

♂

Mandarin is a feral breeder. ♀ has white eye ring and lacks crest. ♂ unmistakable. Mainly ornamental lakes

White patch ▼

White eye stripe

Orange

♂

♀

▲ **Ruddy Duck** is a feral breeder. Small, active diving duck with unique shape. Cocked tail and plumage identify ♂. Shape and behaviour identify ♀. Freshwater bird (rarely marine)

Pink bill

◀ **Egyptian Goose** is a feral breeder in E Anglia. Brown and white head and brown breast patch identify ♂ and ♀

♂

♂

Long legs

♂

Crest

♀

▲ ◀ **Wood Duck** is a feral breeder. Head shape and white eye patch identify ♀

Common Scoter

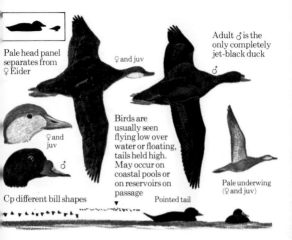

Pale head panel separates from ♀ Eider

♀ and juv

Adult ♂ is the only completely jet-black duck

♂

♀ and juv

♂

Cp different bill shapes

Birds are usually seen flying low over water or floating, tails held high. May occur on coastal pools or on reservoirs on passage ▼

Pointed tail

Pale underwing (♀ and juv)

Usually seen as a snaking line of black dots over the sea, and, in most circumstances, a strictly marine species. Female has brownish plumage, similar to female Eider, but distinguished by different build and bill shape. Feeds by diving for mussels on sea-bed. Seen offshore at all times of year, but principally a winter visitor. A few birds breed in Scotland and Ireland.

Velvet Scoter

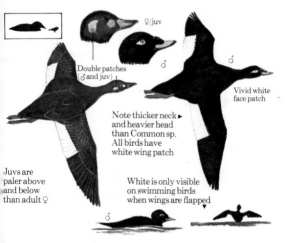

♀/juv

Double patches (♂ and juv) ↑

♂

Vivid white face patch

Note thicker neck ► and heavier head than Common sp. All birds have white wing patch

Juvs are paler above and below than adult ♀

White is only visible on swimming birds when wings are flapped ▼

♂

White wing patches distinguish Velvet Scoter from Common species. Expert diver, like Common Scoter, but favours rougher water. Much less numerous and usually seen in small parties of 15-20. Usually flies low over sea but at great height when migrating. Mainly winter visitor (Sept-May), especially on E coast and W coast from Solway-Anglesey.

Canada Goose

Flies fast with strong, measured beats of its very large wings. Often seen in V-shaped flocks, esp in autumn

Pale breast

White patch contrasting with black neck and head is diagnostic, but note also contrast of black and white below

White neck patch

White

Upperparts are fairly plain brown before autumn moult, but some birds have distinct barring on the back

Dark flanks

White

White chevron

Commonest of the urban park geese. North American species introduced to parks and ornamental lakes in Europe, now well established in Britain and breeding on inland waters throughout Britain (few localities in Ireland). Seen occasionally in coastal areas, but usually grazes inland on marshes or fields near fresh water. Deep "ah huck" flight call.

Barnacle Goose

White face, black neck and breast, grey and black body with mainly grey wings distinguish Barnacle Goose from all other geese ▶

White

Note contrast of black and white on flying bird

Black tail

Grey wing (unlike other geese)

Flocks fly in close but untidy formations

Cream

Distinguished from Canada sp by grey-barred back

Frontal view shows contrast of black and white

Combination of black, white and grey distinguishes from other "black" geese. Juvenile is slightly browner and duller. Grazes on fields and marsh near coast. Rising flocks make great clamour of guttural calls and birds are vocal when swimming. Winter visitor (Oct-Apr), numerous in Hebrides and W and N coast of Ireland. Common in parts of Scotland.

Brent Goose

Pale or white wing-bars distinguish juv birds from adults in the field ◄

White upper tail coverts cover so much of tail that only a thin black line shows at tip. This separates Brent sp from all other geese. Black head and neck and dark flight feathers create black appearance above

Juv

Dark-bellied

Birds often occur in ragged-looking flocks

Dark-bellied

Pale-bellied

Dark-bellied Juv

Dark-bellied

Dark-bellied

Juv birds of both dark and pale-bellied races lack the white nape patch of adults

Pure white

Pale-bellied

Dark-bellied

From rear, undertail shows as solid block of white

Dark-bellied

Note tail-up profile rather like duck

Small, stockily built goose with short tail, neck and bill and comparatively long wings. The two main races, identical apart from their underparts (though a few intermediates may occur), are the pale-bellied race from Canada, Greenland and Scandinavia and the dark-bellied race from N Eurasia. Strictly a marine species and very rare inland. Grazes on salt flats but may up-end in shallows. Normally seen in flight or sitting out at sea but can be very tame, resting in harbours, where unmolested. Flight is fast with wingbeats more rapid than larger relatives and often gathers in irregular flocks wheeling low over coastal flats. Winter visitor (Sept-May) especially to Ireland and E coast of England.

Greylag Goose

Note great contrast ▲ above

Pale grey underwing

Grey rump

Very grey forewing

Greylag has largest head and bill of all "grey" geese.

Grey-brown with pale edges

Eastern race

Pink

Western race

Orange

Pink legs (both races) separate from all ◄ except Pink-footed

Dark spots (Western race)

Largest and heaviest goose, with large head and thick neck very noticeable in flight. Greylag has the palest forewing of all geese. Wingbeats are slower and take-off less agile than in other species. Usually graze for food but may be seen up-ending in shallows. Deep "arhung-ung-ung" call. Widely distributed breeder in British Isles, but is also a winter visitor (Oct-Apr).

White-/Lesser White-fronted Goose

 W

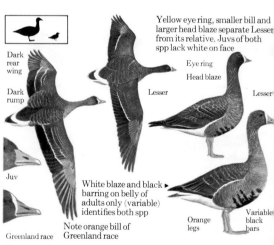

Yellow eye ring, smaller bill and larger head blaze separate Lesser from its relative. Juvs of both spp lack white on face

Dark rear wing

Dark rump

Eye ring

Head blaze

Lesser

Lesser

Juv

White blaze and black ► barring on belly of adults only (variable) identifies both spp

Orange legs

Variable black bars

Greenland race

Note orange bill of Greenland race

White-fronted is a medium-sized, angular-winged, square-headed bird. Lesser White-fronted species is much smaller and shorter necked with larger frontal blaze, and yellow eye ring. Both have shrill calls. Both are winter visitors (Oct-Apr/May). White-fronted Greenland race occurs in W Scotland, Ireland and Severn area. Lesser is rare visitor.

Bean Goose

Cp shape of
head, neck
and bill with
Pink-footed

N Europe

Paler in
imm

Very
dark
(cp Pink-
footed)

Dark head

Adult and imm
of tundra
race are paler

Tundra
race

◄ Upperparts are very dark brown
overall with lighter grey on
outer wing

Head is held high. Orange ►
legs are diagnostic

Pale
yellowish
in imm

Slightly smaller than Greylag, with distinctive erect posture, *long wings, neck and bill. Head and neck are noticeably dark.* Flight is less laboured than Greylag, and neck obtrusive. Feeds with other geese, but is a shy species. Call is louder and deeper than Greylag. Winters regularly in E England in small numbers (Jan-Mar). Odd birds occur elsewhere with other geese.

Pink-footed Goose

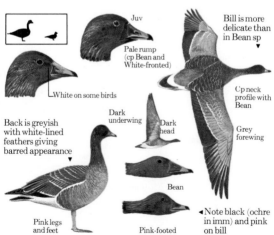

Juv

Bill is more
delicate than
in Bean sp
▼

Pale rump
(cp Bean and
White-fronted)

White on some birds

Cp neck
profile with
Bean

Dark
underwing

Dark
head

Grey
forewing

Back is greyish
with white-lined
feathers giving
barred appearance
▼

Bean

Pink legs
and feet

Pink-footed

◄ Note black (ochre
in imm) and pink
on bill

Delicate birds, particularly in shape of head, very active in flight and on the ground. Highly vocal and may occur in very large flocks. May roost on water or sandbanks. Feeds largely on stubble but cereals, potatoes and grass may be included in diet. Common winter visitor (late Sept-Apr/May) to parts of Scotland, N and E England and Severn estuary.

Swans: Mute, Bewick's and Whooper

Mute

The common swan of park and river, also occasionally seen on the sea. Distinguishable on the water from other swans by the arched neck and wings held raised when swimming, creating a different back profile. May graze on dry and wet meadowland, and up-end in shallows. In flight wings make distinctive throbbing sound. Snorting call. Resident

Mute

Juv Mute

Whooper

Mute-sized but not so heavily built and distinguished by its ringing "whoop-a-hoop" flight call, straighter neck and silent wings. Common winter visitor (Oct-Apr) esp Scotland

Whooper short-necked pose

Bewick's long-necked pose

Bewick's

Smallest of 3 spp, best distinguished from a distance by its size and shorter, thicker neck. Generally similar to Whooper in habits, both spp grazing on grass, but has loud, baying call like pack of hounds. Winter visitor esp to Slimbridge and Ouse Washes. Also occurs in Ireland, but is not common in Scotland

Juv Whooper

Juv Bewick's

Dip in bill

Bewick's

Whooper

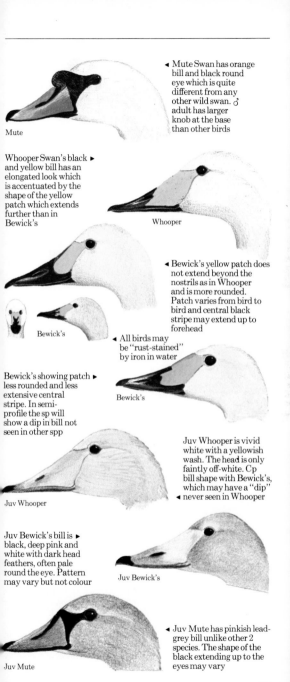

Mute

◀ Mute Swan has orange bill and black round eye which is quite different from any other wild swan. ♂ adult has larger knob at the base than other birds

Whooper Swan's black ▶ and yellow bill has an elongated look which is accentuated by the shape of the yellow patch which extends further than in Bewick's

Whooper

◀ Bewick's yellow patch does not extend beyond the nostrils as in Whooper and is more rounded. Patch varies from bird to bird and central black stripe may extend up to forehead

Bewick's

◀ All birds may be "rust-stained" by iron in water

Bewick's showing patch ▶ less rounded and less extensive central stripe. In semi-profile the sp will show a dip in bill not seen in other spp

Bewick's

Juv Whooper is vivid white with a yellowish wash. The head is only faintly off-white. Cp bill shape with Bewick's, which may have a "dip" ◀ never seen in Whooper

Juv Whooper

Juv Bewick's bill is ▶ black, deep pink and white with dark head feathers, often pale round the eye. Pattern may vary but not colour

Juv Bewick's

◀ Juv Mute has pinkish lead-grey bill unlike other 2 species. The shape of the black extending up to the eyes may vary

Juv Mute

Herring Gull

Larger size, silver-grel upperparts (blue-grey in Common Gull), longer head and heavier bill distinguish Herring from Common Gull. Some winter birds have heavily streaked heads

Winter

Juv is like Lesser Black-backed but tail ◄ pattern separates

In July-Nov many birds show brown wing tips with no white spots ▼

◄ 2nd yr bird (by Nov) shows pale grey back as adult but has dark wings of juv

Typical view of gull ► giving raucous call

Juv

Mediterranean race has darker grey back than British race

Red on bill

British race has pink legs, Mediterranean and Scandinavian have yellow ►

Juv

The typical seaside gull, seen on rooftops and promenades, following ships and wheeling round cliffs along the whole coast of the British Isles. *Larger than Common Gull or Kittiwake,* the other common gulls with grey backs and black wing tips. Adult may be confused with Common sp but heavier build and larger bill distinguishes. Juveniles resemble Lesser Black-backed but latter has darker wings and different tail pattern. Immature birds (second year onwards) progressively show adult markings (grey back in particular). Only grey-backed gull to nest on *rooftops.* Relatively slow, powerful flight. Has the typical echoing gull cry. Resident and probably the most numerous gull in British Isles.

Common Gull

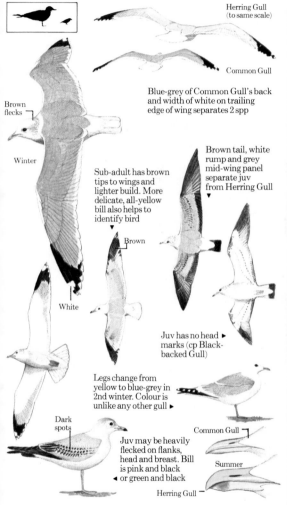

Herring Gull
(to same scale)

Common Gull

Blue-grey of Common Gull's back
and width of white on trailing
edge of wing separates 2 spp

Brown
flecks

Winter

Brown tail, white
rump and grey
mid-wing panel
separate juv
from Herring Gull
▼

Sub-adult has brown
tips to wings and
lighter build. More
delicate, all-yellow
bill also helps to
identify bird
▼

Brown

White

Juv has no head ►
marks (cp Black-
backed Gull)

Legs change from
yellow to blue-grey in
2nd winter. Colour is
unlike any other gull ►

Dark
spots

Common Gull

Juv may be heavily
flecked on flanks,
head and breast. Bill
is pink and black
◄ or green and black

Summer

Herring Gull

"Miniature" Herring Gull, but longer winged and rounder headed with
more delicate bill. *Leg colour of adult is diagnostic* but care is needed to
distinguish it from Kittiwake. Roughly similar in size and plumage,
Kittiwake has very long, thin wings and different distribution of black and
white on wing tips. Leisurely flight, more buoyant than Herring Gull.
Shriller call than Herring Gull. Less of a marine species than the Herring
Gull, rarely seen any distance out to sea. Common breeding bird in
Scotland, N England and N and W Ireland, and in winter is very
frequently seen on agricultural land, playing fields and in urban centres
generally throughout British Isles.

171

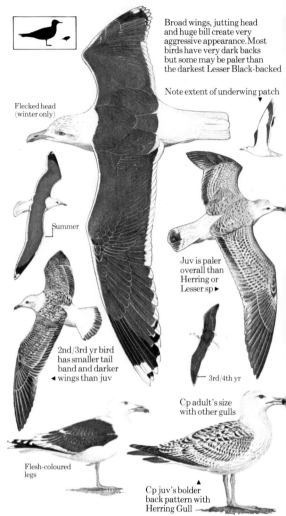

Broad wings, jutting head and huge bill create very aggressive appearance. Most birds have very dark backs but some may be paler than the darkest Lesser Black-backed

Note extent of underwing patch ▼

Flecked head (winter only)

Summer

Juv is paler overall than Herring or Lesser sp ►

2nd/3rd yr bird has smaller tail band and darker ◄ wings than juv

3rd/4th yr

Cp adult's size with other gulls

Flesh-coloured legs

Cp juv's bolder back pattern with Herring Gull ▲

Largest of all gulls, dwarfing other gulls on ground and with a wide wingspan. A fierce predator, taking seabirds and young during breeding season (particularly Puffins and Shearwaters) and an imposing scavenger at other times. Size and appearance should identify, but birds at a distance may be difficult to tell from Lesser Black-backed species. Although adults have dark back and wings, juveniles are whiter on head, paler above with less brown on tail than Lesser Black-backed and Herring Gulls. Flight looks slow and ponderous but birds are fast enough to hunt down crippled birds. Deepest call of the gulls. Breeds Scotland, Ireland, and W and S coast of England and occurs commonly inland.

Lesser Black-backed Gull

Juv is darker than ► juv Herring Gull, esp in tail, outer wing and trailing edge. Note slim build and long, narrow wings

◄ Plumage pattern is almost identical to larger Great Black-backed's (cp bird to same scale opposite), but note darker grey

Flecked head (winter only)

Cp juv with juv Herring Gull ▼

Juv

Sub adult

1st/2nd yr

Juv ▲ Herring Gull

Juv

◄ Yellow legs in adult distinguish from pink-legged Great Black-backed

British (summer)

Cp British race (summer) with Scandinavian

Scandinavian (winter)

Smaller than Herring Gull with *more delicate head and longer, thinner wings and considerably smaller than Great Black-backed Gull*, but combination of plumage similarities and difficulties of judging size can make two black-backed species confusable at a distance. Plumage varies considerably but the long projection of wings beyond tail at rest separates from Herring Gull. In flight the slimmer build will distinguish it from Great Black-backed. Juvenile Lesser Black-backed's darker plumage should distinguish from juvenile Herring Gull. The darker Scandinavian race occurs as winter migrant. Common bird inland outside breeding season (Aug-Apr) on reservoirs and in urban areas.

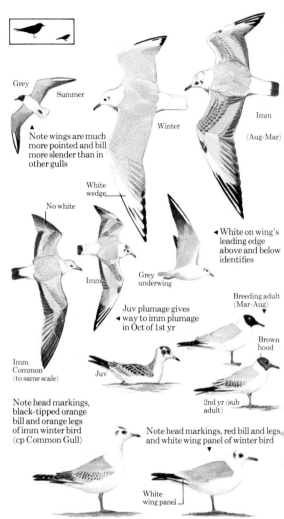

Grey

Summer

Note wings are much more pointed and bill more slender than in other gulls

Winter

Imm (Aug-Mar)

White wedge

No white

White on wing's leading edge above and below identifies

Imm

Grey underwing

Juv plumage gives way to imm plumage in Oct of 1st yr

Breeding adult (Mar-Aug)

Brown hood

Imm Common (to same scale)

Juv

Note head markings, black-tipped orange bill and orange legs of imm winter bird (cp Common Gull)

2nd yr (sub adult)

Note head markings, red bill and legs, and white wing panel of winter bird

White wing panel

Smallest of the commonly seen gulls with a noticeably slender build and pointed wings. Combination of *red or orange legs and red bill are seen on no other gull* (but compare with terns). Distinctive black, white and grey pattern on wings (particularly white triangle on upper wing) and *brown hood on summer birds* make identification easy. Imm also shows white leading edge on wing but tail, unlike that of adult, has a pronounced dark band. Flight is much lighter and more effortless than the larger gulls. *Harsh, screeching "kwarrk" and "kick" call.* Occurs commonly inland particularly on arable land. Also breeds far inland throughout the British Isles, though less widespread in S England and S Ireland.

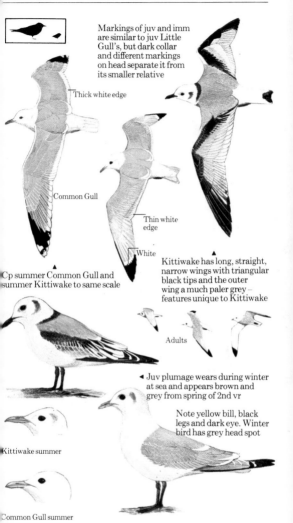

Markings of juv and imm are similar to juv Little Gull's, but dark collar and different markings on head separate it from its smaller relative

Thick white edge

Common Gull

Thin white edge

White

Cp summer Common Gull and summer Kittiwake to same scale

Kittiwake has long, straight, narrow wings with triangular black tips and the outer wing a much paler grey – features unique to Kittiwake

Adults

Juv plumage wears during winter at sea and appears brown and grey from spring of 2nd yr

Note yellow bill, black legs and dark eye. Winter bird has grey head spot

Kittiwake summer

Common Gull summer

Most marine of the gulls, but increasingly common throughout Britain. At close range, combination of black and yellow bill on adult distinguishes from all other gulls. *Slimmer wing shape and distinctive wing markings on adult and young birds distinguish it from larger Common Gull.* Birds pick food from the surface in flight, or settle on water and then dive. They may also plunge from a height like a tern. Flight is fairly fast with shallow wingbeats. *Diagnostic "kitiwaka" call.* Nests in dense colonies on cliffs, and now also breeds in groups on buildings. Very rarely seen inland (only storm-driven birds), and few birds are seen in winter, which most birds spend far out at sea.

Little Gull

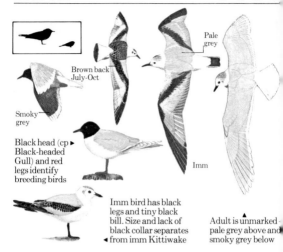

Pale grey

Brown back July-Oct

Smoky grey

Black head (cp Black-headed Gull) and red legs identify breeding birds ►

Imm

Imm bird has black legs and tiny black bill. Size and lack of black collar separates ◄ from imm Kittiwake

Adult is unmarked pale grey above and ▲ smoky grey below

Smallest of the gulls, and easy to distinguish from them by size alone, but leisurely, dipping, Tern-like flight can make it difficult to pick out in a flock of Terns. Juvenile has white underwing like Kittiwake but brown back identifies. Seen round all coasts of British Isles but also occurs inland, spring, autumn and winter. Increasing.

Fulmar

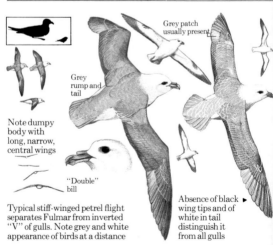

Grey patch usually present

Grey rump and tail

Note dumpy body with long, narrow, central wings

"Double" bill

Typical stiff-winged petrel flight separates Fulmar from inverted "V" of gulls. Note grey and white appearance of birds at a distance

Absence of black ► wing tips and of white in tail distinguish it from all gulls

Size of Common Gull but plumage pattern, body and bill shape, together with typical banking, rising and falling petrel flight, distinguish it from all gulls. Follows trawlers for offal. Breeds on all suitable cliffs around coast of British Isles, and also nests on buildings. May be seen off most beaches, especially those with headlands, even where not breeding.

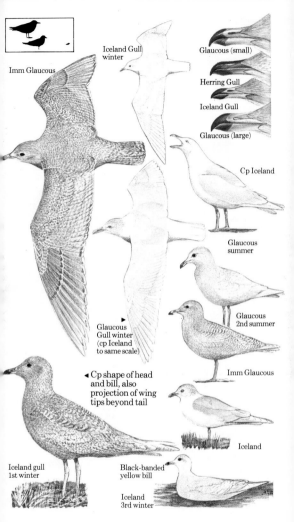

Iceland Gull
winter

Imm Glaucous

Glaucous (small)

Herring Gull

Iceland Gull

Glaucous (large)

Cp Iceland

Glaucous
summer

▶ Glaucous
Gull winter
(cp Iceland
to same scale)

Glaucous
2nd summer

◀ Cp shape of head
and bill, also
projection of wing
tips beyond tail

Imm Glaucous

Iceland

Iceland gull
1st winter

Black-banded
yellow bill

Iceland
3rd winter

Adults of both species vary from pale grey to white and lack any black in wing. In all plumages wing tips are paler than rest of wing. Most Glaucous Gulls are ponderous, pot-bellied birds, about the size of the Great Black-backed Gull, but small Glaucous Gulls may be seen. These small birds are roughly the same size as the Iceland Gull (i.e. about Herring Gull size) and the two species may be very difficult indeed to distinguish. Iceland has more delicate head and bill than small or large Glaucous, with wing tips extending beyond its tail. Both are winter visitors (Oct-Apr), but Glaucous is more common than the Iceland Gull, occurring in numbers around Shetland with individuals annually in S England.

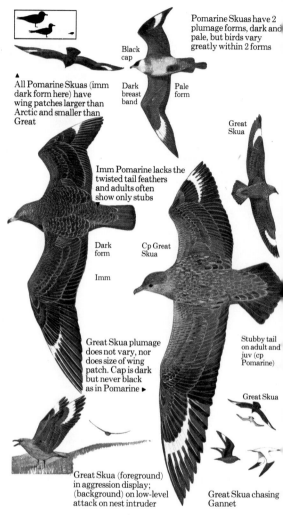

All Pomarine Skuas (imm dark form here) have wing patches larger than Arctic and smaller than Great

Pomarine Skuas have 2 plumage forms, dark and pale, but birds vary greatly within 2 forms

Black cap

Dark breast band

Pale form

Great Skua

Imm Pomarine lacks the twisted tail feathers and adults often show only stubs

Dark form

Cp Great Skua

Imm

Great Skua plumage does not vary, nor does size of wing patch. Cap is dark but never black as in Pomarine ▶

Stubby tail on adult and juv (cp Pomarine)

Great Skua

Great Skua (foreground) in aggression display; (background) on low-level attack on nest intruder

Great Skua chasing Gannet

Great Skua is largest of the skuas. A powerful bird with slow, ponderous-looking flight, but agile in the pursuit of birds from which it "pirates" food. Except in the breeding season, when it moves to open moorland in colonies, it will only be seen out at sea. Breeds N coast Scotland, Orkney, Shetland and Hebrides. Passage migrant seen in Apr and especially Aug-Oct. The Pomarine is between Great and Arctic species in size. *Tail of adults is diagnostic*, although juveniles and immatures may be difficult to distinguish from Arctic Skua. On passage, has typical heavy flight with steady wingbeats. Passage migrant Apr and Sept-Oct, especially off coasts of SE England and N Scotland.

Arctic Skua

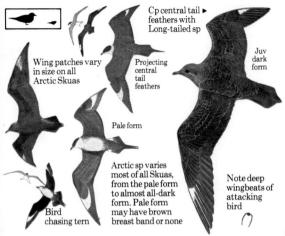

Cp central tail ▶
feathers with
Long-tailed sp

Juv
dark
form

Wing patches vary
in size on all
Arctic Skuas

Projecting
central
tail
feathers

Pale form

Arctic sp varies
most of all Skuas,
from the pale form
to almost all-dark
form. Pale form
may have brown
breast band or none

Note deep
wingbeats of
attacking
bird

Bird
chasing tern

The most widespread of the skuas along the coast of the British Isles.
*Medium-sized bird with robust, sharply etched profile. Shape, size and build
together with tail shape identify species. Fast, flapping flight is interspersed
with glides, giving bird falcon-like appearance.* Breeds from SW coast
Scotland up to Shetland. Passage migrant in spring and autumn.

Long-tailed Skua

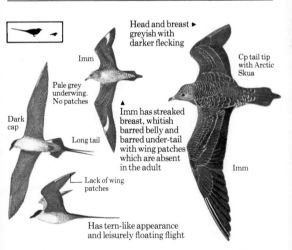

Head and breast ▶
greyish with
darker flecking

Imm

Cp tail tip
with Arctic
Skua

Pale grey
underwing.
No patches

Dark
cap

▲
Imm has streaked
breast, whitish
barred belly and
barred under-tail
with wing patches
which are absent
in the adult

Long tail

Imm

Lack of wing
patches

Has tern-like appearance
and leisurely floating flight

*Smallest, most delicately built Skua, with wings longer and thinner in
proportion than Arctic Skua and more delicate head and bill.* Flight lacks the
falcon-like energy of Arctic species. Second year sub-adult's tail tips only
as long as adult Arctic. Passage migrant rare in spring but occurs in Sept-
Oct, especially E coast England and NW coast Scotland

Common Tern

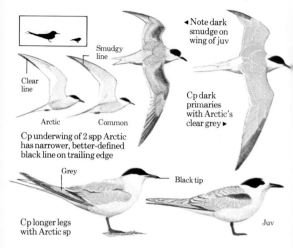

Note dark smudge on wing of juv ◄

Smudgy line

Clear line

Arctic   Common

Cp underwing of 2 spp Arctic has narrower, better-defined black line on trailing edge

Cp dark primaries with Arctic's clear grey ►

Grey

Black tip

Cp longer legs with Arctic sp

Juv

Most widespread breeding tern in British Isles. *Black-tipped, orange-red bill and longer red legs distinguishes* from Arctic Tern. Size of transparent area on wing (only small in Common Tern) is diagnostic. Dives for fish. Grating "kee-errrr" call. Summer visitor, breeds in colonies on coast or inland waters. (Apr-Nov, few birds in Nov.)

Arctic Tern

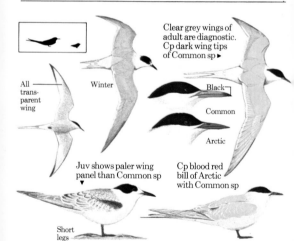

Clear grey wings of adult are diagnostic. Cp dark wing tips of Common sp ►

All transparent wing

Winter

Black

Common

Arctic

Juv shows paler wing panel than Common sp ▼

Cp blood red bill of Arctic with Common sp

Short legs

Easily confused with Common Tern, but spring birds tend to be much greyer below than Common. *Blood-red bill and very short legs identify Arctic. Transparent outer wing is also diagnostic.* Flight and behaviour identical to Common Tern. Nests around coasts of Britain and inland in Ireland. Also occurs inland on passage, Apr-June and Aug-Oct passage.

Roseate Tern

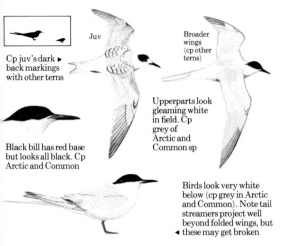

Juv

Broader wings (cp other terns)

Cp juv's dark ► back markings with other terns

Upperparts look gleaming white in field. Cp grey of Arctic and Common sp

Black bill has red base but looks all black. Cp Arctic and Common

Birds look very white below (cp grey in Arctic and Common). Note tail streamers project well beyond folded wings, but ◄ these may get broken

Vivid whiteness (pink flush may sometimes be seen on body), *black bill and broader, shorter wings should distinguish from Common or Arctic.* Seen from below, wing tip also lacks dark border. Wingbeats are shallower than Arctic or Common. *Distinct "tchewick" call, together with a rasping "haaaak".* Summer visitor (Apr-Sept), (rare breeder). Very rare inland.

Little Tern

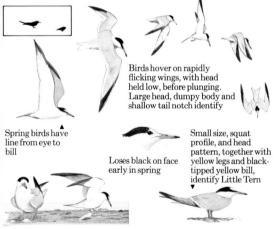

Birds hover on rapidly flicking wings, with head held low, before plunging. Large head, dumpy body and shallow tail notch identify

Spring birds have line from eye to bill

Loses black on face early in spring

Small size, squat profile, and head pattern, together with yellow legs and black-tipped yellow bill, identify Little Tern

Smallest of the terns by far, with long, angular wings and no tail streamers. At close range, *yellow bill is diagnostic* but hurried-looking flight and prolonged hovering identify at a distance. *Sharp "kit-kit" and grating "kree-ick" call.* Breeds along coasts of British Isles, nesting on beach in very exposed situations. Summer visitor (Apr-Oct).

181

Sandwich Tern

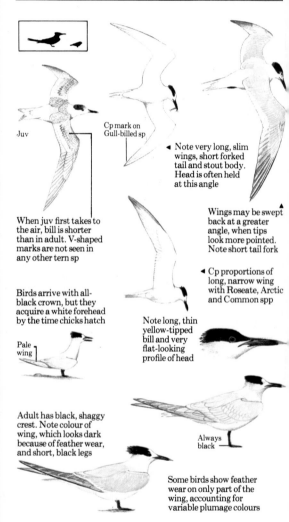

Juv

Cp mark on Gull-billed sp

◀ Note very long, slim wings, short forked tail and stout body. Head is often held at this angle

Wings may be swept back at a greater angle, when tips look more pointed. Note short tail fork

When juv first takes to the air, bill is shorter than in adult. V-shaped marks are not seen in any other tern sp

◀ Cp proportions of long, narrow wing with Roseate, Arctic and Common spp

Birds arrive with all-black crown, but they acquire a white forehead by the time chicks hatch

Note long, thin yellow-tipped bill and very flat-looking profile of head

Pale wing

Adult has black, shaggy crest. Note colour of wing, which looks dark because of feather wear, and short, black legs

Always black

Some birds show feather wear on only part of the wing, accounting for variable plumage colours

Largest of the common breeding terns, with a different structure from other four species. *At all times, long, black, yellow-tipped bill, shaggy head, black legs, and long, angular wings identify.* Noticeably whiter-looking than Common and Arctic Terns. Flight is more powerful than smaller species, with deliberate wingbeats, and wing proportions (Sandwich has a longer "arm") also create a distinctive flight action. Plunges for fish (especially sand eels). *Has distinct, loud "skee-rick" call* and birds may be seen calling excitedly as they fly over, holding catch. Summer visitor (Apr-Oct), nesting in colonies around coasts of British Isles. Occasionally, passage birds occur inland (especially Aug-Sept).

Black Tern

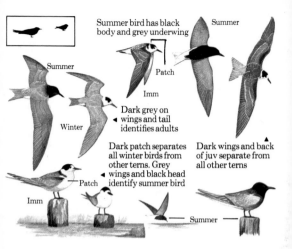

Summer bird has black body and grey underwing

Summer

Patch

Imm

Summer

Dark grey on ◄ wings and tail identifies adults

Winter

Dark patch separates all winter birds from other terns. Grey ◄ wings and black head identify summer bird

Dark wings and back ▲ of juv separate from all other terns

Imm

Patch

Summer

A marsh tern with distinctive dipping flight to catch insects (never dives like sea terns). *Black head and body and extent of grey on wings of summer bird* distinguish species. Black cap and *dark patch extending from nape* distinguish winter adults and young birds from all other terns. Rarely settles on water. Summer visitor (Apr-Oct).

White-winged Black Tern

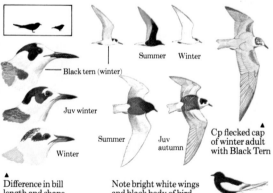

Black tern (winter)

Summer   Winter

Juv winter

Winter

Summer

Juv autumn

Cp flecked cap of winter adult with Black Tern

▲ Difference in bill length and shape of 2 spp shows at a distance. Cp areas of black and white

Note bright white wings and black body of bird in summer. Square brown back and white rump identify autumn juv

A marsh tern with startling contrast of black and white in summer which easily identifies it. *Bill and tail are shorter and wings broader than in Black Tern. Bill length and white underwing identify winter birds* but Cp Whiskered Tern (winter). Annual but scarce visitor in spring and autumn, both coastal and inland, usually with Black Terns.

Seabirds

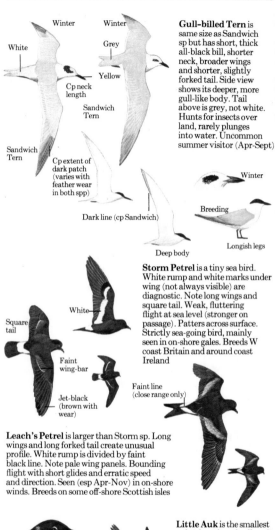

Gull-billed Tern is same size as Sandwich sp but has short, thick all-black bill, shorter neck, broader wings and shorter, slightly forked tail. Side view shows its deeper, more gull-like body. Tail above is grey, not white. Hunts for insects over land, rarely plunges into water. Uncommon summer visitor (Apr-Sept)

Winter

White

Winter

Grey

Yellow

Cp neck length

Sandwich Tern

Sandwich Tern

Cp extent of dark patch (varies with feather wear in both spp)

Dark line (cp Sandwich)

Deep body

Winter

Breeding

Longish legs

Storm Petrel is a tiny sea bird. White rump and white marks under wing (not always visible) are diagnostic. Note long wings and square tail. Weak, fluttering flight at sea level (stronger on passage). Patters across surface. Strictly sea-going bird, mainly seen in on-shore gales. Breeds W coast Britain and around coast Ireland

White

Square tail

Faint wing-bar

Jet-black (brown with wear)

Faint line (close range only)

Leach's Petrel is larger than Storm sp. Long wings and long forked tail create unusual profile. White rump is divided by faint black line. Note pale wing panels. Bounding flight with short glides and erratic speed and direction. Seen (esp Apr-Nov) in on-shore winds. Breeds on some off-shore Scottish isles

Winter

Longer in all Razorbills

Razorbill

Winter

Summer

Little Auk is the smallest auk (about length of hand). Appears short, stout and neckless on water. Wings extend beyond tail (cp Razorbill). White flecks on back are diagnostic (cp Razorbill, esp juv). Bill looks minute. Flight is strong and whirring. Winters at sea (seen in on-shore gales)

Caspian Tern is enormous (same size as Herring Gull) with huge, orangy-red bill, all black or white-flecked cap and short, forked tail. Proportions of wing create gull-like profile. Flight is powerful. Dives like other tern spp. Deep, crow-like call. Occasional visitor to British Isles (Apr-Oct), usually on rivers or reservoirs inland

Dark

Huge bill

Grey or dark (varies with wear)

Black feet

Non-breeding plumage

Winter

Mediterranean Gull is larger, with heavier head and bill and broader wings than Black-headed sp. Note white wings of adults and black hood of summer birds. Mainly marine but also inland. Increasing and regular visitor to England

Juv

Sub-adult

Black

Grey panel (cp Common Gull)

White wing

Summer

Black head

White eye ring

Dark

Dark grey

White cheeks

Black

Whiskered Tern is a marsh sp. Contrasting plumage pattern of summer bird, with black cap, white cheeks and dark grey underparts, is unique. Upperparts are pearly grey. Care is needed to separate winter birds from White-winged Black Tern in winter plumage. Summer visitor to fresh-water marshes in Europe. Rare in British Isles

Short forked tail

Summer

Winter

185

Manx Shearwater

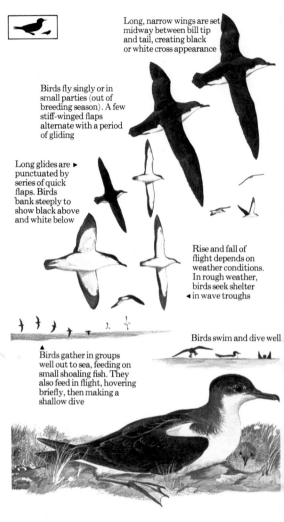

Long, narrow wings are set midway between bill tip and tail, creating black or white cross appearance

Birds fly singly or in small parties (out of breeding season). A few stiff-winged flaps alternate with a period of gliding

Long glides are ► punctuated by series of quick flaps. Birds bank steeply to show black above and white below

Rise and fall of flight depends on weather conditions. In rough weather, birds seek shelter ◄ in wave troughs

Birds swim and dive well

▲ Birds gather in groups well out to sea, feeding on small shoaling fish. They also feed in flight, hovering briefly, then making a shallow dive

Large flocks of Manx Shearwater appear as flashing black and white crosses, flying close to the surface of the sea or, in fresh winds, rising and falling above the waves. *Plumage, stiff-winged flight and cruciform profile distinguish species from all other sea birds round British coasts.* Birds travel long distances to feed far out to sea, coming ashore only during the breeding season to nest in burrows, mainly on islands offshore. Birds arrive and leave the burrow in the dark to avoid predation by gulls. During breeding, loud, cacophonous screams indicate presence. Breeding colonies are scattered round the W coast of Britain, from the Shetlands to the Scillies, and around the Irish coast.

Razorbill

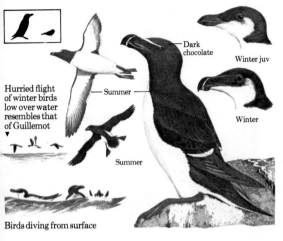

Dark chocolate

Winter juv

Winter

Hurried flight of winter birds low over water resembles that of Guillemot ▼

Summer

Summer

Birds diving from surface

Short, deep bill, heavy head and thick neck, together with *jet black and white plumage* identify the Razorbill. On water, long wing tips and pointed tail create pointed silhouette at rear. Sits high in water and dives showing wing and tail tips as it goes under. Nests with Guillemots on cliffs and stacks round coasts of British Isles (absent from Humber to Isle of Wight).

Guillemot

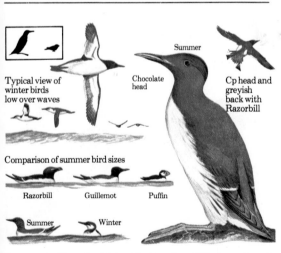

Summer

Typical view of winter birds low over waves

Chocolate head

Cp head and greyish back with Razorbill

Comparison of summer bird sizes

Razorbill   Guillemot   Puffin

Summer   Winter

Commonest of the auks. *Distinguished from Razorbill by larger size and slender, dagger-shaped bill.* British birds can be identified by grey upperparts, but Northern race, which may winter with local birds, looks as black as Razorbill and is best identified by shape. Flight is fast and low with rapid whirring wingbeats. Breeding and distribution as Razorbill.

Black Guillemot

"Bridled" summer

"Bridled" winter

Summer ▶

Guillemot

"Bridled" birds occur more commonly in northern colonies

Autumn

Brünnich's Guillemot

Summer

Juv

Summer bird has white underwing and upper wing patch

Red feet

Yellow feet

Summer

Winter

Smaller than the Guillemot. White on wings makes summer adults unmistakable and shape, combined with *whitish upperparts, identifies winter birds.* Normally seen on the water but rests on rocks. Nests in holes under rocks, breeding in small groups around coasts of Ireland, W Wales and Scotland and on islands offshore. Most birds are sedentary.

Puffin

Puffins are at home in the highest seas, often bouncing over waves to take off

Flight is strong with rapid wingbeats

Multicoloured bill and face pattern are unique

Juv

Winter

Summer

Note bill ◀ change

Small size, bill shape, and dumpy black and white body distinguishes Puffin from other auks. Bill changes in shape and colour during winter. Flight is fast for a heavy bird, and usually low over waves. Birds sit high in water and dive well. Breeds in cliff-top burrows in places scattered round coasts of British Isles, particularly in Scotland and Scottish isles. Winters at sea.

Shag

Adult breeding birds have bottle-green plumage with a crest which is often raised. In winter birds are browner and lack the crest

Yellow gape (breeding birds)

Typical view of Shag in breeding plumage with crest raised. Note thin bill

Imm Cormorant

Imm Shag

Shag has slimmer bill and often rounded head

Imm birds have brownish, patchy underparts and differ from young Cormorants, which usually have a pure white belly

Both Shag and Cormorant extend their wings to dry, but Shag stretches its wings out farther

Both species fly low over water and land awkwardly, but Shag has more rapid wingbeats and is more often seen singly

Shag looks all dark on water

Cormorant

White

Shag dives with a noticeable jump

Large, black-looking bird with a distinctive profile both at rest and in flight, to be seen around rocky coasts of the British Isles. Normally a strictly marine species, frequenting open water rather than the more sheltered waters and estuaries of the Cormorant, and breeding on rocks and in caves, but may occasionally be seen inland after gales. *Markedly smaller, slimmer-necked and more slender-billed than the Cormorant* with oily, sleek appearance. Dives expertly and may surface some distance away. Absent as breeder from part of SE and E coast N to Flamborough, otherwise breeds on all suitable rocky coasts and islands in British Isles N to Shetland. Some birds disperse along coasts in winter.

Cormorant

Breeding birds of the Southern race show more white

Larger and longer ► winged than Shag. Birds occur inland, often soaring to great heights

Imm

◄ Imm birds in 2nd winter have less white on the head than any other Cormorant. Cp amount of yellow with bill of imm Shag

White throat

◄ Cp wing-drying posture with Shag. Also dries wings on water

Breeding birds are bronze above and steel-blue below, with white patches

White (breeding season only)

▲ Kinked neck and rather stiff flight profile create prehistoric look

2nd winter

▲ Big fish are eaten on surface

Imm

Profiles are similar but cp head and bill

Shag

Cormorant

Imm Cormorant

Shag

Large, ungainly birds, typically seen perched erect and unmoving on a buoy or pier or flying low and fast over the water. *Adults are distinguishable at all times of year from the very similar Shag by their larger size, and by white on face and chin.* Young birds show variable plumage and are more difficult to indentify, but their whitish underparts distinguish them from the young Shag. Behaviour and flight are very similar to Shag, and, like the Shag, species is a colonial nester. Found on coasts, like the Shag, but commonly occurs on inland rivers and large areas of water including urban reservoirs. Breeds on rocks on the coast and in trees inland. Coastal distribution is similar to Shag.

Gannet

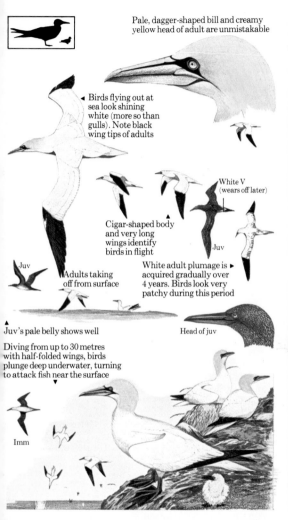

Pale, dagger-shaped bill and creamy yellow head of adult are unmistakable

◀ Birds flying out at sea look shining white (more so than gulls). Note black wing tips of adults

White V (wears off later)

Cigar-shaped body and very long wings identify birds in flight

Juv

Juv

Adults taking off from surface

White adult plumage is ▶ acquired gradually over 4 years. Birds look very patchy during this period

Juv

▲ Juv's pale belly shows well

Head of juv

Diving from up to 30 metres with half-folded wings, birds plunge deep underwater, turning to attack fish near the surface ▼

Imm

Largest European sea bird, unmistakable in its dazzling black and white plumage. Almost always in the air, resting on the water only briefly after feeding. Often seen from shore, usually fairly well out to sea. Sometimes birds may fly low over waves when travelling some distance, but will also soar to considerable heights, following coastline. *Wings flex noticeably at tips in flight.* Several deep flaps are followed by a glide on angled wings. Found inland only after storms, usually on ground. Seen off all coasts of British Isles, especially in spring and autumn, with most birds dispersing to southern oceans in winter. Breeds on cliffs and stacks, mainly on offshore islands, round coasts of British Isles.

Birdwatcher's Checklist

Upperparts

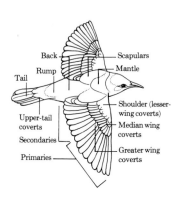

Underparts

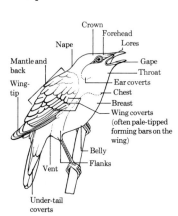

Size *Cp with other sp (if possible)*

Head *Shape, crest, plumage pattern*

Bill *Size, shape, colour*

Upperparts *Streaked, spotted, barred, plain*

Underparts *Streaked, spotted, barred, plain*

Wing
Length *Extended, folded (relative to tail)*
Breadth *Extended*
Markings *Upper wing, Underwing*

Tail *Shape, length, markings*

Legs *Length, colour*

Actions
Flight *Swift/medium/slow*
Direct/undulating
Ground *Walks/ hops/ runs/ perches/ wades/ swims/ dives*

Calls *Repetitive/ varied/single note Harsh/melodious*

Place

Habitat

Time of year

Useful Organizations and Publications

Royal Society for the Protection of Birds, The Lodge, Sandy, Bedfordshire SG19 2DL. Mainly concerned with bird protection, habitat conservation, research and education. Controls large number of reserves. Publishes *Birds* magazine quarterly. Open membership.

The British Trust for Ornithology, Beech Grove, Tring, Hertfordshire HP23 5NR. Mainly concerned with research into bird population and movements and ecology. Publishes journals, pamphlets and guides. Open membership.

The Wildfowl Trust, Slimbridge, Gloucester GL2 7BT. Mainly concerned with the conservation and study of wildfowl. Open membership.